A CONCISE ELEMENTARY GRAMMAR OF THE SANSKRIT LANGUAGE

A CONCISE ELEMENTARY GRAMMAR OF THE SANSKRIT LANGUAGE

WITH EXERCISES, READING SELECTIONS, AND A GLOSSARY

Second Edition

BY

JAN GONDA

TRANSLATED FROM THE GERMAN
BY
GORDON B. FORD, JR.

THE UNIVERSITY OF ALABAMA PRESS
Tuscaloosa

Published by The University of Alabama Press, 2006

∞
The paper on which this book is printed meets the minimum requirements of American National Standard for Information Science—Permanence of Paper for Printed Library Materials, ANSI Z39.48-1984.

Library of Congress information available at the Library of Congress

ISBN-13 978-08173-5261-5 (alk. paper)
ISBN-10 0-8173-5261-9

CONTENTS

TRANSLATOR'S PREFACE

I have translated the fourth edition of Professor Jan Gonda's excellent textbook, *Kurze Elementar-Grammatik der Sanskrit-Sprache* (Leiden, E. J. Brill, 1963), for use in my elementary Sanskrit course at Northwestern University, which is designed primarily for linguists who wish to acquire a knowledge of Sanskrit grammar as rapidly as possible. Professor Gonda's book is ideal for this purpose. The grammar is presented in a clear and thorough way and is accompanied by twenty useful translation exercises. In addition, there are thirteen well chosen reading selections and a Sanskrit-English glossary containing every word which occurs in the translation exercises and reading selections.

I should like to express my thanks to Professor Gonda for his kindness in reading the manuscript of my translation in its entirety. In addition, I am extremely grateful to Professor Frithjof A. Raven for many helpful suggestions.

Evanston, February 1966. GORDON B. FORD, JR.

THE SCRIPT

The most common of the Indic alphabets is the devanāgarī script, in which the individual signs as a rule express not only a vowel or only a consonant but a consonant with following vowel. The vowel which follows is ă if it is not specially designated. The devanāgarī alphabet is thus a syllabic script.

Consonant Signs with Following ă

Velars	क	ख	ग	घ	ङ
	ka	kha	ga	gha	ṅa
Palatals	च	छ	ज	झ	ञ
	ca	cha	ja	jha	ña
Linguals	ट	ठ	ड	ढ	ण
	ṭa	ṭha	ḍa	ḍha	ṇa
Dentals	त	थ	द	ध	न
	ta	tha	da	dha	na
Labials	प	फ	ब	भ	म
	pa	pha	ba	bha	ma
Semivowels	य	र	ल	व	
	ya	ra	la	va	
Sibilants	श	ष	स		
	śa	ṣa	sa		
Aspirate	ह				
	ha				

The visarga ḥ is designated by a colon after the preceding letter: सः = saḥ; the anusvāra ṃ by a dot over the preceding letter: तं = taṃ. ṃ and ḥ stand before k in the alphabet or, if they represent a nasal or sibilant, in the place of these symbols.

If the vowels stand in initial position and are not joined with the preceding consonant, then they are designated by the following signs:

अ a, आ ā, इ i, ई ī, उ u, ऊ ū, ऋ ṛ, ॠ ṝ, ऌ ḷ,
ए e, ऐ ai, ओ o, औ au.

If vowels other than ă are joined to the above symbols, then they are represented in the following way:

ा	ā	e.g.	का kā, धा dhā, या yā
ि	i	e.g.	चि ci ति ti यि yi
ी	ī	e.g.	नी nī, भी bhī, यी yī
ु	u	e.g.	कु ku, रु ru, शु or शु śu
ू	ū	e.g.	रू rū, हू hū, शू or शू śū
ृ	ṛ	e.g.	कृ kṛ, धृ dhṛ, हृ hṛ
ॄ	ṝ	e.g.	कॄ kṝ, तॄ tṝ, हॄ hṝ
े	e	e.g.	के ke, ते te, ये ye

ै ai e g कै kai, तै tai, षै ṣai

ो o e.g. को ko, चो co, भो bho

ौ au e.g. तौ tau, नौ nau, यौ yau

ॢ ḷ e.g. कॢ kḷ, मॢ mḷ

The omission of an initial a is designated by the avagraha ऽ, e.g.: ते ऽपि te 'pi.

If a consonant without vowel is to be designated, then this is done by means of a stroke ्, called a virāma; e.g.: क् k, प् p, म् m.

If in a word or sentence two or more consonants immediately follow one another, then the above signs are joined in one group (ligature).

If the first of the consonants to be joined ends on the right with a vertical stroke, then it is placed first with loss of this stroke: न् n + त ta: न्त nta.

If the first consonant does not end with the vertical stroke, then the following consonant is joined under the preceding one with loss of its horizontal stroke: क् k + व va: क्व kva.

Exceptions: न na and ल la as the second members of a ligature are usually placed underneath with loss of their horizontal stroke; म ma and य ya are in this case written after the first sign and in a more shortened form (s. below). Note also kta, ktha, kṣa, chya, jña, ñca, ñja, ṇṇa, tta, dda, ddha, dna, dbha, pta, hna, hva.

r before a cons. and before ṛ is designated by a hook placed above (ʳ); the latter stands completely to the right: rka: र्क. r after a cons. is represented by a stroke placed under it: pra: प्र. Especially to be noted: tra: त्र. More than two consonants are joined according to the same rules; s. below.

List of the most common ligatures:

क्क kka, क्ख kkha, क्त kta, क्त्य ktya, क्त्र ktra, क्त्व ktva, क्थ ktha, क्न kna, क्म kma, क्य kya, क्र kra, क्ल kla, क्व kva, क्ष kṣa, क्ष्म kṣma, क्ष्य kṣya, क्ष्व kṣva — ख्य khya, ख्र khra — ग्द gda, ग्ध gdha, ग्न gna, ग्भ gbha, ग्म gma, ग्य gya, ग्र gra, ग्र्य grya, ग्ल gla, ग्व gva — घ्न ghna, घ्म ghma, घ्य ghya, घ्र ghra — ङ्क ṅka, ङ्क्ष ṅkṣa, ङ्ग ṅga, ङ्घ ṅgha, ङ्म ṅma.

च्च cca, च्छ ccha, च्छ्र cchra, च्छ्व cchva, च्ञ cña, च्म cma, च्य cya — छ्य chya, छ्र chra — ज्ज jja, ज्ज्व jjva, ज्झ jjha, ज्ञ jña, ज्ञ्य jñya, ज्म jma, ज्य jya, ज्र jra, ज्व jva — ञ्च ñca, ञ्छ ñcha, ञ्ज ñja.

ट्क ṭka, ट्ठ ṭṭha, ट्य ṭya — ठ्य ṭhya, ठ्र ṭhra — ड्ग ḍga, ड्य ḍya — ढ्म ḍhma, ढ्य ḍhya — ण्ट ṇṭa, ण्ठ ṇṭha, ण्ड ṇḍa, ण्ढ ṇḍha ण्ण or ण्ण ṇṇa, ण्म ṇma, ण्य ṇya, ण्व ṇva.

त्क tka, त्त tta, त्त्य ttya, त्त्र ttra, त्त्व ttva, त्थ ttha, त्न tna, त्प tpa, त्म tma, त्म्य tmya, त्य tya, त्र tra, त्त्र ttra, त्र्य trya, त्व tva, त्स tsa, त्स्न tsna, त्स्य tsya — थ्य thya — द्ग dga, द्ग्य dgya, द्ग्र dgra, द्द dda, द्द्र ddra, द्द्व ddva, द्ध ddha, द्ध्न ddhna, द्ध्य ddhya, द्न dna, द्ब dba, द्भ dbha, द्भ्य dbhya, द्म dma. द्य dya, द्र dra, द्र्य drya, द्व dva, द्व्य dvya — ध्न dhna, ध्म dhma, ध्य dhya, ध्र dhra, ध्व dhva — न्त nta, न्त्य ntya, न्त्र ntra, न्थ ntha, न्द nda, न्द्ध्य nddhya, न्द्द्र nddra, न्ध ndha, न्ध्र ndhra, न्न nna, न्म nma, न्य nya, न्र nra, न्व nva, न्स nsa.

प्त pta, प्त्य ptya, प्न pna, प्म pma, प्य pya, प्र pra, प्ल pla, प्स psa — फ्य phya — ब्ज bja, ब्द bda, ब्ध bdha, ब्न bna, ब्ब bba, ब्भ bbha, ब्र bra — भ्य bhya, भ्र bhra — म्न mna, म्प mpa, म्ब mba, म्भ mbha, म्य mya, म्र mra, म्ल mla.

य्य yya, य्व yva — र्क rka, र्ज rja, र्ध rdha — ल्क lka, ल्य lya, ल्ल lla, ल्व lva — व्य vya, व्र vra.

श्च or श्च śca, श्न śna, श्य or श्य śya, श्र śra, श्र्य śrya, श्ल śla, श्व śva, श्व्य śvya — ष्क ṣka, ष्क्र ṣkra, ष्ट ṣṭa, ष्ट्य ṣṭya, ष्ट्र ṣṭra, ष्ट्र्य ṣṭrya, ष्ट्व ṣṭva, ष्ठ ṣṭha, ष्ठ्य ṣṭhya,

ष्ण ṣṇa, ष्ण्य ṣṇya, ष्प ṣpa, ष्प्र ṣpra, ष्म ṣma, ष्य ṣya, ष्व ṣva — स्क ska, स्ख skha, स्त sta, स्त्य stya, स्त्र stra, स्त्व stva, स्थ stha, स्न sna, स्प spa, स्फ spha, स्म sma, स्म्य smya, स्य sya, स्र sra, स्व sva,.

ह्ण hṇa, ह्न hna, ह्म hma, ह्य hya, ह्र hra, ह्ल hla, ह्व or ह्व hva.

Symbols for the numerals

१	२	३	४	५	६	७	८	९	०
1	2	3	4	5	6	7	8	9	0

१९४० 1940

Word division. Within a sentence word division occurs if a word ends in a vowel, anusvāra or visarga and the following word begins with a cons., just as according to §§ 7-9; 15. Otherwise either phonetic fusion or union into one syllabic sign occurs with observance of the pertinent sandhi rules.

Punctuation. This script depends solely on । for the designation of a minor sentence segment or the end of a half strophe, and on ॥ to designate a large segment or the end of a strophe.

READING EXERCISE

अस्माकं मुद्रणालये वेद-वेदान्त-धर्मशास्त्र-प्रयोग-
asmākaṃ mudraṇālaye veda-vedānta-dharmaśāstra-prayoga-

योग-सांख्य-ज्योतिष-पुराणेतिहास-वैद्यक-मंत्र-स्तोत्र-
yoga-sāṃkhya- jyotiṣa-purāṇetihāsa-vaidyaka-maṃtra-stotra-

कोश-काव्य-चम्पू-नाटकालंकार-संगीत-नीति-कथाग्रंथाः
kośa-kāvya-campū-nāṭakālaṃkāra-saṃgīta-nīti-kathāgraṃthāḥ,

बहवः स्त्रीणां चोपयुक्ता ग्रंथाः बृहज्ज्योतिषार्णवनामा
bahavaḥ strīṇāṃ copayuktā graṃthāḥ, bṛhajjyotiṣārṇavanāmā

बहुविचित्रचित्रितोऽयमपूर्वग्रन्थः । संस्कृतभाषया
bahuvicitracitrito 'yam apūrvagranthaḥ. saṃskṛtabhāṣayā

हिन्दीमार्वाड्यन्यतरभाषाग्रन्थास्तत्तच्छास्त्राद्यर्थानु-
hindīmārvāḍyanyatarabhāṣāgranthāstattacchāstrādyarthānu-

वादकाः चित्राणि पुस्तकमुद्रणोपयोगिन्यो यावत्यस्सा-
vādakāḥ citrāṇi pustakamudraṇopayoginyo yāvatyassā-

मग्र्यः स्वस्वलौकिकव्यवहारोपयोगिचित्रचित्रितालि-
magryaḥ svasvalaukikavyavahāropayogicitracitritāli-

खितपत्रवत्पुस्तकानि च मुद्रयित्वा प्रकाशन्ते सुलभेन
khitapatravatpustakāni ca mudrayitvā prakāśante sulabhena

मूल्येन विक्रयाय । येषां यत्राभिरुचिस्तत्तत्पुस्तकाद्यु-
mūlyena vikrayāya. yeṣāṃ yatrābhirucistattatpustakādyu-

पलब्धय एवं नव्यतया स्वस्वपुस्तकानि मुमुद्रयि-
palabdhaya evaṃ navyatayā svasvapustakāni mumudrayi-

षुभिः सुलभयोग्यमौल्येन सीसकाक्षरैः स्वच्छोत्त-
ṣubhiḥ sulabhayogyamaulyena sīsakākṣaraiḥ svacchotta-

मोत्तमपत्रेषु मुद्रिततत्पुस्तकानां स्वस्वसमयानुसारे-
mottamapatreṣu mudritatatpustakānāṃ svasvasamayānusāre-

णोपलब्धये च पत्रिकाद्वारातैः प्रेषणीयो ऽस्मि ॥
ṇopalabdhaye ca patrikādvārātaiḥ preṣaṇīyo ’smi

PHONOLOGY

§ 1. VOWELS. *a ā i ī u ū ṛ ṝ ḷ*
e ai o au

ā ī ū ṝ are long, also the monophthongized diphthongs *e* (from *ai*) and *o* (from *au*), likewise *ai* and *au*, which continue *āi* and *āu*.

CONSONANTS:

	Voiceless Stops Unaspir.	Voiceless Stops Aspir.	Voiced Stops Unaspir.	Voiced Stops Aspir.	Nasals (voiced)
Velars	*k*	*kh*	*g*	*gh*	*ṅ*
Palatals	*c*	*ch*	*j*	*jh*	*ñ*
Cerebrals (Linguals)	*ṭ*	*ṭh*	*ḍ*	*ḍh*	*ṇ*
Dentals	*t*	*th*	*d*	*dh*	*n*
Labials	*p*	*ph*	*b*	*bh*	*m*
Semivowels (voiced)			*y*	*r*	*l* *v*
Sibilants (voiceless)			*ś* (palat.)	*ṣ* (cerebr.)	*s* (dent.)
Aspirate (voiced)			*h*		
(Secondary Phonetic Symbols)			*ḥ*	*ṃ*	◡

§ 2. PRONUNCIATION. If not otherwise noted, the sounds are so pronounced as they are reproduced here in Latin transcription.

ṛ ṝ ḷ are syllabic, *ṛ ḷ* are pronounced like *er*, *el* in German *Vater*, *Engel*, with a slight *i* as an off-glide. The aspirates are pronounced with a clearly audible aspiration following quickly afterward; *ph* thus does not equal *f*! The *ṅ* is English *ng* in *sing*. The *c* is pronounced like English *ch* in *church, j* as in English *justice, ñ* like the French palatalized *n* (written *gn*). The cerebrals are pronounced like the dentals, but with a reflexed tip of the tongue, thus like English *t*, etc. The semivowels *y* and *v* are to be pronounced like German *j* and *w* (somewhat more like English *w*). *ś* is approximately German *ch* in *ich*; it lies between *ß* in *beißen* and *sch* in *Schall*; *ṣ* is a cerebral *sch*, approximately French *ch* without lip rounding; *s* is always sharp dental *s*, never *z*! The visarga (*ḥ*) is a light voiceless aspirate; at the end of a sentence the preceding vowel occurs as an off-glide. The anusvāra *ṃ*, a nasal lengthening of the vowel, can be pronounced before semivowels, sibilants, and *h* like final *n* in French (e.g. *Jean*); otherwise it is pronounced internally in words like the nasal of the same class (thus before *k g* like *ṅ*, etc.); in word-final position it is usually *m*. The anunāsika (◡̇ or ~) occurs only in combination with *l*, in order to express nasalized *l*.

Accentuation. In the contemporary pronunciation the rule of accentuation valid for Latin is extended to the last four syllables of a word. A certain stress thus rests on the penultimate syllable if this is long by nature or by position (two consonants following the vowel), on the antepenultimate syllable if the penultimate is short and it itself is long, otherwise—thus if the penultimate and antepenultimate syllables are short—on the fourth-to-last syllable. Examples: *utkṣípya, vā́nara, mūrkhéṇa, ṭíṭṭibhī* (*bh* is a single cons.), *udvéjayati, ábhihitaḥ*. In compounds each component usually retains its own accentuation.

§ 3. Changes of Vowels by Gradation (Ablaut).

Vowels are subject to a double gradation in inflection and word formation.

Weak grade	—	*i* (*ī*)	*u* (*ū*)	*ṛ* (*ṝ*)	*ḷ*
Full grade, Guṇa	*a*	*e* (from *ai*)	*o* (from *au*)	*ar*	*al*
Lengthened grade, Vṛddhi	*ā*	*ai* (from *āi*)	*au* (from *āu*)	*ār*	—

Examples: *pa-pt-ima* "we fell"; *pat-ati* "he falls": *pāt-ayati* "he causes to fall".

diś- [1]) "direction, region": *deś-a-* "place, region": *daiś-ika-* "local, acquainted with a locality".

tul-ā "scales": *tol-ana-* "weighing": *taul-in-* "weigher".

kṛ-ta- "made": *kar-tṛ-* "doer": *kār-ya-* "business".

kḷp-ta- "being in order": *kalp-ate* "be in order".

Root vowels which occur in long closed syllables are practically excluded from this gradation; thus: *nindati* "he reproves" always remains *nind-*, *jīv-ati* "he lives": *jīv-*.

§ 4. Vowels and consonants in absolute final position.

I. As a rule there remains only the first of two or more consonants which should end a word: *bharan* "bearing" has arisen from **bharant-s* [2]). The combinations *rk*, *rṭ*, *rt*, *rp* nevertheless occur in final position.

II. In the final position of a word at the end of a sentence or verse occur only: vowels and diphthongs (except *ṛ*, *ṝ*, and *ḷ*), the voiceless, non-aspirated stops (except *c*), the nasals (except *ñ*), *ḥ*, and *l*. The remainder, if they originally or according to § 4 I are supposed to occur in final position, undergo the following changes·

[1]) Word stems and roots are distinguished by an added -.

[2]) * designates a form not attested but reconstructed.

III. The voiced stops and aspirates, except the palatals, change to the corresponding voiceless stops: *tat* "this" from *tad*; *pat* "foot" from **pad-s*, *triṣṭup* "name of a prosodic meter" from **triṣṭubh-s*.

IV. The palatal stops change to *k*, *j* sometimes to *ṭ*; *ñ* becomes *ṅ*: *vāk* "voice" from **vāc-s*, *srak* "garland" from **sraj-s*, *devarāṭ* "king of the gods" from **devarāj-s*.

V. *ś* shifts to *k* or *ṭ*, *ṣ* and *h* become *ṭ*, more rarely *k*: *dik* "region" stands for **diś-s*, to the stem *madhulih-* "bee" belongs the nom. sg. *madhuliṭ*.

VI. *r* and *s* become *ḥ* after vowels: *devaḥ* "god" from *devas*, *punaḥ* "again" from *punar*.

Note: If root syllables which begin with a voiced stop (*g*, *d*, *b*) and end in a voiced aspirate (thus *gh*, *dh*, *bh*) or *h* change the final consonant, then the original aspiration of the initial sound appears: *budh-* "awakening": n. sg. *bhut* from **bhudh-s*; likewise *bhotsyate* "he will awaken" from **bhodh-*, root in Old Ind. *budh-*, originally *bh(a)udh*; but *bodh-ate* "he awakens".

§§ 5-17. PHONETIC CHANGE IN THE SENTENCE (SANDHI).

In the connection of sentences and in the formation of compounds the final sound of a preceding word and the initial sound of the following word undergo the following changes: [1])

§ 5. CONTACT OF FINAL AND INITIAL VOWELS.

I. Simple similar [2]) vowels coalesce to form the corresponding long vowel:

---

[1]) In the following rules the form of the words in absolute final position is generally taken as the starting point. They are thus practical rules, not rules of historical development.

[2]) Similar vowels are vowels which are not distinguished or are distinguished only by their quantity.

a or *ā* + *a* or *ā* becomes *ā*: *na asti* > [1]) *nāsti* "is not", *na āste* > *nāste,* "does not sit".

i or *ī* + *i* or *ī* becomes *ī*: *nadī iva* > *nadīva* "like a river", *yadi īśvarah* > *yadīśvaraḥ* "if the lord".

u or *ū* + *u* or *ū* becomes *ū*: *sādhu uktam* > *sādhūktam* "well spoken".

II. *a* and *ā* merge with simple dissimilar vowels to produce their full grade (cf. § 3): thus:

a or *ā* + *i* or *ī* becomes *e*: *ca ihi* > *ceha* "and here", *tvā īśvara* > *tveśvara* "you, O lord".

a or *ā* + *u* or *ū* becomes *o*: *ca uktam* > *coktam* "and said", *sā uvāca* > *sovāca* "she said".

a or *ā* + *ṛ* or *ṝ* becomes *ar*: *kva ṛṣiḥ* > *kvarṣiḥ,* "where the ṛṣi?", *yathā ṛṣiḥ* > *yatharṣiḥ* "like a ṛṣi".

III. *a* and *ā* merge with diphthongs to produce their lengthened grade:

a or *ā* + *e* or *ai* becomes *ai*: *ā eti* > *aiti* comes here", *ca* + *aiti* > *caiti* "and comes".

a or *ā* + *o* or *au* becomes *au*: *sā oṣadhiḥ* > *sauṣadhiḥ* "the medicinal herb", *tadā* + *aughaḥ* > *ta-*

---

[1]) > means "becomes"; < means "derives from".

daughaḥ "then the flood".

§ 6. THE VOWELS *i, u, ṛ, ī, ū, ṝ* before dissimilar vowels shift to the corresponding semivowel, thus to *y, v, r*: *yadi etat* > *yady etat* "if this", *astu evam* > *astv evam* "be it so".

§ 7. Before vowels other than *a* final *e* and *o* become *a* with hiatus: *vane āste* > *vana āste* "he sits in the forest", *prabho ehi* > *prabha ehi* "O lord, come".

e and *o* remain unchanged before initial *a*, but the *a* is elided: *te atra* > *te 'tra* "these (pl.) here", *so api* > *so 'pi* "he also" (s. also § 48).

§ 8. *ai* before vowels as a rule changes to *ā*, *au* to *āv*: *asmai adāt* > *asmā adāt* "to this one he gave", *putrau ubhau* > *putrāv ubhau* "the two sons".

§ 9. EXCEPTIONS TO §§ 5-8. The endings *ī, ū, e* of dual forms remain unchanged before vowels and effect no elision.

§ 10. FINAL VOICELESS STOPS. The voiceless stop as in absolute final position (§ 4) remains only before voiceless consonants. Before a voiced initial sound (thus also before a vowel or semivowel) a voiced stop appears instead of the voiceless stop, before an initial nasal the final voiceless or voiced stop is changed into the nasal of its class: *pattanāt āgacchati* > *pattanād āgacchati* "he comes from the city"; *dik-* + *jaya-* > *digjaya-* "conquest of all regions"; *vāk me* > *vāṅ me* "my speech"; *tat namas* "the respect" > *tan namas* (sometimes also *tad namas*).

§ 11. Final *t* of the form in absolute final position is assimilated to an initial palatal, cerebral, or *l*: *tat ca* > *tac ca* "and this", *tat janma* > *taj janma* "this birth", *tat lebhe* > *tal lebhe* "I obtain this". Final *t* and *d* with initial *ś* go to *cch*: *tat śrutvā* > *tac chrutvā* "having heard this".

§ 12. FINAL NASALS.

I. Final *n* before *j* changes to *ñ*: *tān janān* > *tāñ janān* "these people (acc.)", before *ḍ* to *ṇ*, before *ś* to *ñ*, in which case the *ś* usually becomes *ch*: *tān śrutvā* > *tāñ śrutvā* or *tāñ chrutvā* "having heard them". Before *l* it becomes *ṃl* or ̐*l*: *balavān loke* > *balavā̐l loke* (*balavāl̐ loke*) "mighty in the world".

II. Before a following *c*, *ṭ*, *t* either an original *s* has been preserved after the final *n* of the form in absolute final position or an *s* is inserted analogically; this *s* is assimilated to *ś* before *c*, to *ṣ* before *ṭ*; the *n* becomes *ṃ* (anusvāra): **bharant-s ca* > *bharaṃś ca* "and bearing", **aśvāns tadā* > *aśvāṃs tadā* "then horses"; *kasmin cin nagare* > *kasmiṃś cin* (or *kasmiṃścin*) *nagare* "in some town or other".

III. Final *m* which remains unchanged before vowels becomes anusvāra before consonants: *kṛtam ca* > *kṛtaṃ ca* "and made", *sam* + *gacchanti* > *saṃgacchanti* "they come together". We also find *sandhi-* beside *saṃdhi-*, etc.

IV. Final nasals except *m* are doubled after a short vowel before an initial vowel: *san atra* > *sann atra* "being here", *pratyaṅ āste* > *pratyaṅṅ āste* "he is sitting toward the west".

§§ 13-16. FINAL *r*, *s*, *ḥ*.

§ 13. Instead of *s* and *r* is found the *ḥ* of the form in absolute final position (§ 4 VI) also before *k*, *kh*, *p*, *ph*, *ś*, *ṣ*, *s*: *tisraḥ kanyāḥ* "3 girls", *punaḥ pratiṣṭhati* "he goes away again", *pūjitaḥ Śivaḥ* "Śiva is revered"; *muktaḥ syāt* "let him be freed".

Note. Sometimes final *s* is assimilated before *ś*, *ṣ*, or *s*: *Indraś śūraḥ* "Indra the hero"; *muktas syāt.*

Before *c* and *ch* appears instead of *s*, *r* (form in absolute final position *ḥ*): *ś*; before *ṭ* and *ṭh*: *ṣ*; before *t* and *th* *s* remains unchanged and *s* appears instead of *r*: *devas ca* > *devaś ca* "and the god"; *punar ca* > *punaś ca* "and again"; *devas tatra* "the god there"; *punar tatra* > *punas tatra* "again there".

§ 14. Before initial voiced sounds *r* stands instead of *s*, *r* after vowels except *a* and *ā*: *avis mama* > *avir mama* "my sheep", *dhenus iva* > *dhenur iva* "like a cow", *guṇais yuktaḥ* > *guṇair yuktaḥ* "provided with virtues".

Note. The particle *bhoḥ* becomes *bho* before all voiced sounds.

§ 15. *as* becomes *o* before voiced consonants and before *a* (which disappears); thus *devas gacchati* > *devo gacchati* "a god is coming", *devas api* > *devo 'pi* "also a god"; form in absolute final position *devaḥ* (§ 4, VI).

Before vowels other than *a*, *as* in this case becomes *a* with hiatus, thus *aśvas iva* > *aśva iva* "like a horse", *devas uvāca* > *deva uvāca* "the god spoke".

Note. *sas* and *eṣas* (§ 48) lose their *s* before every consonant: *eṣa siṃhaḥ* "this lion".

ās becomes *ā* before all voiced sounds, before vowels with hiatus: *aśvās vahanti* > *aśvā vahanti* "the horses travel", *Damayantyā niveśanam* "the dwelling of D.", *devā ūcuḥ* "the gods spoke".

§ 16. *r* disappears before initial *r* with compensatory lengthening of the preceding short vowel: *punar rājati* > *punā rājati* "he distinguishes himself again"; also an *r* originating from *s* (§ 14): *nṛpatis ramate* > *nṛpatī ramate* "the king enjoys himself". Cf. also: *śanakai rājā . . . abravīt* "the king spoke very calmly" (*śanakai* instead of *śanakais*, form in absolute final position *śanakaiḥ*).

§ 17. INITIAL CONSONANTS. The combination: final voiceless stop and initial *h* results in voiced stop and voiced aspirate: *etat hi* > *etad dhi* "for this", *srak hi* > *srag ghi* "for a garland".

Initial *ch* becomes *cch* after a short vowel, after *mā* "not", and after the preposition *ā* "to": *bhavati chāyā* > *bhavati cchāyā* "it is shade".

Note. Internally in words after vowels we find instead of *ch*: *cch*: *chid-* "split": *ciccheda*.

§§ 18-20. SOUND CHANGES IN THE INTERIOR OF A WORD.

The rules §§ 5-17 also apply to the contact of the final sound of a root with the initial sound of a suffix, of the final sound of a stem with the initial sound of a personal ending or of a case ending, etc. But there are some exceptions; the most important are:

§ 18. CHANGES OF VOWELS.

I. In some cases, namely in monosyllabic words and after a double consonant, we find instead of *i* and *ī*: *iy*, and instead of *u* and *ū*: *uv*: *dhī-* "thought": *dhiyam* (acc. sg.), *bhū-* "earth": *bhuvā* (instr. sg.).

II. Before a following vowel and *y* appears instead of *e*: *ay*, instead of *ai*: *āy*, instead of *o*: *av*, instead of *au*: *āv*: *e-mi* "I go": *ay-āni* "I want to go" (§ 3), *go-bhis* (instr. pl.) "with the cattle": *gavām* (gen. pl.) "of the cattle", *nau-s* (n. sg.) "ship": *nāv-am* (acc. sg.).

III. Before radical *r* + cons. and *v* + cons. *i* and *u* are usually lengthened: *pur-* "city": dat. pl. *pūr-bhyas*.

§ 19. I. CONSONANTS remain unchanged before suffixes and endings which begin with vowel, semivowel, or nasal: *tapas-e* dat. sg. of *tapas-* "asceticism", *tapas-vin-* "ascetic", but *tapo-nidhi-* "ascetic" (from *tapas-nidhi-*), since this is a compound.

Before other consonants the final consonant is treated according to the rules of the form in absolute final position (§ 4), and further according to §§ 10 ff., with which it should be noted that before a voiceless consonant voiced stops become voiceless, aspirated stops shift to the unaspirated voiceless stops; before a voiced consonant the aspirated stops become unaspirated voiced stops. Examples: *manas-* "mind": loc. pl. *manaḥ-su* according to § 13; instr. pl. *mano-bhis* according to § 15; *sraj-* "garland": loc. pl. *srak-ṣu*.

III. If a root or a stem ends in a voiced aspirate and a suffix or an ending begins with *t* or *th*, then this is changed to *d* and receives the aspiration: *labh-ta-* > *lab-dha-* "obtained". From the roots beginning with *d* and ending in *h* forms with *-gdh-* are formed: *duh-* "milk": *dugdha-* "milked"; likewise from *snih-* "love": *snigdha-*; but cf. VII.

IV. Dentals become cerebral after cerebrals: *dviṣ-* "hate": *dveṣ-ti* > *dveṣṭi* "he hates".

V. *c*, *j*, *ś* are treated as in final position (§ 4 IV, V); but before *t* or *th* *j* is often changed to *ṣ* and *ś* always is: *dṛś-ta-* > *dṛṣṭa-* "seen", but *yuj-ta* > *yukta-* "bound".

VI. According to § 4 V and § 20 II *ṣ* + *s* becomes *kṣ*; *ś* + *s* is also represented by *kṣ*.

VII. Instead of *h* with following *t, th, dh* we find *ḍh*, with which a preceding short vowel except *ṛ* is lengthened as in *lih* + *tha* > *līḍha* "you lick" (2nd pl. pres. ind., § 64 IV), etc.

VIII. Before sibilants *n* and *m* become anusvāra, *m* before other consonants except *y* becomes *n*: *han* + *si* > *haṃsi* "you kill"; *gam* + *tum* > *gantum* "to go".

IX. *n* becomes *ñ* after *c* and *j*: *rāj-nā* > *rājñā* (§ 39); *yaj-na-* > *yajña-* "sacrifice".

§ 20. I. An *n* which a vowel or *n m y v* follows is changed to *ṇ* if *ṛ ṝ r ṣ* immediately precede in the same word or no palatal, cerebral, or dental stands in between: *muṣ-nā-ti* > *muṣṇāti* "he steals"; *karman-ā* > *karmaṇā* "by the deed", but *rathena* "by the chariot"; *śuśrūṣaṇa-* "obedience", *sravaṇa-* "flowing", but *darśana-* "seeing", *grasana-* "swallowing".

II. An *s* is changed to *ṣ* if *k r* or a vowel other than *a ā* precedes immediately or is separated only by *ḥ* or *ṃ* and a sound other than *ṛ r* follows: *sthā-* "stand": *tiṣṭhati* "he stands"; *dhenu-* "cow": *dhenuṣu* loc. pl.; but *tisras* "three (fem.)".

DECLENSION

Preliminary remarks. Sanskrit has three genders: masculine, feminine, neuter; three numbers: singular, dual (expressing the number two), plural; eight cases: nominative, vocative, accusative, instrumental, dative, ablative, genitive, locative (cf. § 114).

The case endings of the neuters deviate from the masculines only in the nom., voc., and acc. of the three numbers. The endings are given below. One distinguishes: a) the vocalic declension; here the stem ends in a vowel; b) the consonantal declension: the stem ends in a consonant.

VOCALIC DECLENSION

§ 21. Stems in *a*; masculines and neuters.

Masculines. Paradigm: *aśva-* "horse".

	Singular	Dual	Plural
Nom.	*aśvas*	*aśvau* (Nom., Voc., Acc.)	*aśvās* (Nom., Voc.)
Voc.	*aśva*		
Acc.	*aśvam*		*aśvān*
Instr.	*aśvena*	*aśvābhyām* (Instr., Dat., Abl.)	*aśvais*
Dat.	*aśvāya*		*aśvebhyas* (Dat., Abl.)
Abl.	*aśvāt*		
Gen.	*aśvasya*	*aśvayos* (Gen., Loc.)	*aśvānām*
Loc.	*aśve*		*aśveṣu* (§ 20 II)

Neuters. Paradigm: *dāna-* "gift". Like the masculines, only nom. acc. voc. sg. *dānam*, n.a.v. du. *dārei*, n.a.v. pl. *dānāni*.

§ 22. STEMS IN *ā*; feminines.

Paradigm: *senā-* "army".

Nom.	*senā*		
Voc.	*sene*	*sene*	*senās*
Acc.	*senām*		
Instr.	*senayā*		*senābhis*
Dat.	*senāyai*	*senābhyām*	*senābhyas*
Abl. / Gen.	*senāyās*		
			senānām
Loc.	*senāyām*	*senayos*	*senāsu*

Like §§ 21, 22 also the adjectives in *a*, fem. *ā*; e.g. *nava-* "new": masc. *navas*, neutr. *navam*, fem. *navā*. Several adjectives, however, form the feminine stem with the suffix *ī* (§ 27).

Note. The acc. sing. neutr. of an adj. is frequently used with adverbial meaning: *śīghra-* "quick", adverb *śīghram*.

STEMS IN *i* AND *u*; masc., fem., and neuters.

§ 23. MASCULINES. Paradigms: *ali-* "bee", *paśu-* "cattle".

Sg.	Du.	Pl.	Sg.	Du.	Pl.
alis		*alayas*	*paśus*		*paśavas*
ale	*alī*		*paśo*	*paśū*	
alim		*alīn*	*paśum*		*paśūn*
alinā		*alibhis*	*paśunā*		*paśubhis*
alaye	*alibhyām*	*alibhyas*	*paśave*	*paśubhyām*	*paśubhyas*
ales		*alīnām*	*paśos*		*paśūnām*
	alyos			*paśvos*	
alau		*aliṣu*	*paśau*		*paśuṣu*

One should note: a) *pati-* "lord, master": sing. n. *patis*, v. *pate*, a. *patim*, i. *patyā*, d. *patye*, ab. g. *patyus* (*patyur*, § 14), l. *patyau*; at the end of a compound it is inflected like *ali-*: *bhūpataye* (dat.) "to the lord of the earth".

b) *sakhi-* "friend": sing. n. *sakhā*, v. *sakhe*, a. *sakhāyam*, i. *sakhyā*, d. *sakhye*, ab. g. *sakhyus* (*sakhyur*, as above), l. *sakhyau*, du. *sakhāyau*, *sakhibhyām*, *sakhyos*, pl. *sakhāyas*, *sakhīn*, etc. like *ali-*.

§ 24. Neuters. Paradigms: *vāri-* "water", *madhu-* "honey".

NVA	*vāri*	*vāriṇī*	*vārīṇi*	*madhu*	*madhunī*	*madhūni*
I.	*vāriṇā*	*vāribhyām*	*vāribhis*	*madhunā*	*madhubhyām*	*madhubhis*
D.	*vāriṇe*		*vāribhyas*	*madhune*		*madhubhy*
Ab.	*vāriṇas*			*madhunas*		
G.		*vāriṇos*	*vārīṇām*		*madhunos*	*madhūnān*
L.	*vāriṇi*		*vāriṣu*	*madhuni*		*madhuṣu*

§ 25. Feminines. Paradigms: *gati-* "going", *dhenu-* "cow"; cf. also §§ 23 and 27.

	Sg.	Pl.	Sg.	Pl.
N.	*gatis*	*gatayas*	*dhenus*	*dhenavas*
V.	*gate*		*dheno*	
A.	*gatim*	*gatīs*	*dhenum*	*dhenūs*
I.	*gatyā*	*gatibhis*	*dhenvā*	*dhenubhis*
D.	*gataye, gatyai*	*gatibhyas*	*dhenave, dhenvai*	*dhenubhyas*
Ab.	*gates, gatyās*		*dhenos, dhenvās*	
G.		*gatīnām*		*dhenūnām*
L.	*gatau, gatyām*	*gatiṣu*	*dhenau, dhenvām*	*dhenuṣu*

The dual like *ali-* and *paśu-*, § 23.

§ 26. THE ADJECTIVES IN *i* AND *u* are declined like the substantives, except that the n. can also have the forms of the masc. in the d. ab. g. l. sg. and in the g. l. du.: *śuci-* "pure": g. sg. n. *śucinas* and *śuces*; *tanu-* "thin": d. sg. n. *tanune* and *tanave*. Adjectives in *u* can also form their feminine with *ū* or by addition of the suffix *-ī-* (inflected according to § 27); some feminines have two or all three of these forms, e.g., *tanu*: f. *tanu-*, *tanū-*, *tanvī-*.

§ 27. STEMS IN *ī* AND *ū*; feminines.

Polysyllabic stems. Paradigms: *nadī-* "river", *vadhū-* "woman".

Sg.	Du.	Pl.	Sg.	Du.	Pl.
nadī	*nadyau*	*nadyas*	*vadhūs*	*vadhvau*	*vadhvas*
nadi			*vadhu*		
nadīm		*nadīs*	*vadhūm*		*vadhūs*
nadyā	*nadībhyām*	*nadībhis*	*vadhvā*	*vadhūbhāam*	*vadhūbhis*
nadyai		*nadībhyas*	*vadhvai*		*vadhūbhya*
nadyās	*nadyos*	*nadīnām*	*vadhvās*	*vadhvos*	*vadhūnām*
nadyām		*nadīṣu*	*vadhvām*		*vadhūṣu*

Note. The word *lakṣmī-* "luck" and name of a goddess, and some other words have *īs* in the n. sg.: *lakṣmīs*.—The feminines of the stems ending in consonants follow this inflection: *balin-* "strong": fem. *balinī-*, *mahat-* "great": fem. *mahatī-*, as do the fem. beside a part of the stems in *a*: *deva-* "god": *devī-* "goddess" (cf. § 22), optionally the adjectives in *u*: *tanu-* "thin": *tanvī-* (s. § 26), the stems of the nouns of agent in *tṛ* (s. § 29): *dātṛ-* "giver": fem. *dātrī-*.

§ 28. MONOSYLLABIC FEMININES. Paradigms: *dhī-* "thought", *bhū-* "earth".

	Sg.	Pl.	Sg.	Pl.
N.	*dhīs*	*dhiyas*	*bhūs*	*bhuvas*
V.				
A.	*dhiyam*		*bhuvam*	
I.	*dhiyā*	*dhībhis*	*bhuvā*	*bhūbhis*
D.	*dhiye, dhiyai*	*dhībhyas*	*bhuve, bhuvai*	*bhūbhyas*
Ab.	*dhiyas, dhiyās*		*bhuvas, bhuvās*	
G.		*dhiyām, dhīnām*		*bhuvām, bhūnām*
L.	*dhiyi, dhiyām*	*dhīṣu*	*bhuvi, bhuvām*	*bhūṣu*

du. *dhiyau, dhībhyām, dhiyos*; *bhuvau, bhūbhyām, bhuvos.*

Note. The word *strī-* "woman" is inflected: sg. n. *strī*, v. *stri*, a. *striyam, strīm*, d. *striyai*, ab. g. *striyās*, l. *striyām*; pl. n. acc. *striyas, strīs*, g. *strīṇām*, otherwise like *dhī-*.

§ 29. STEMS IN *r*; nouns of agent (masc. and n.); words for relationship (masc. and fem.); cf. the preliminary remark to §§ 36-45.

Nouns of agent in *tṛ*. Paradigm: *dātṛ-* "giver".

	Sg.	Du.	Pl.
N.	*dātā*	*dātārau*	*dātāras*
V.	*dātar*		
A.	*dātāram*		*dātṝn*
I.	*dātrā*	*dātṛbhyām*	*dātṛbhis*
D.	*dātre*		*dātṛbhyas*
Ab.	*dātur* (§ 4 VI)		
G.		*dātros*	*dātṝṇām*
L.	*dātari*		*dātṛṣu*

The paradigm of the infrequent neuters corresponds exactly to the neuter *i-* and *u-*stems: sg. *dātṛ, dātṛṇā, dātṛṇe*, etc., du. *dātṛṇī*, etc., pl. *dātṝṇi, dātṛbhis*, etc. Concerning the fem.: § 27.

The words for relationship *naptṛ-* "grandson", *bhartṛ-* "husband", *svasṛ-* f. "sister" are inflected like *dātṛ-*, thus e.g., *svasā, svasāram, svasrā*, etc.; pl. acc. *svasṝs*.

§ 30. THE REMAINING WORDS FOR RELATIONSHIP have *a* instead of *ā* in the acc. sg., in the n.v. acc. du. and in the n. pl., thus: *pitā, pitar, pitaram*, etc., *pitarau*, etc., *pitaras*, etc.; *mātṛ-* "mother" has *mātṝs* in the acc. pl.

Of *nṛ-* "man" only the n. *nā* is in use in the sg.; the remaining cases are formed from the *a*-stem *nara-*; in the g. pl. *nṛṇām* is also found beside *nṝṇām*.

§ 31. STEMS IN DIPHTHONGS.

Only the words *nau-* "ship" and *go-* "cow" occur frequently. Inflection: sg. n.v. *naus*, a. *nāvam*, i. *nāvā*, d. *nāve*, ab. g. *nāvas*, l. *nāvi*; du. *nāvau, naubhyām, nāvos*; pl. n.v.a. *nāvas*, i. *naubhis*, d. ab. *naubhyas*, g. *nāvām*, l. *nauṣu*; sg. *gaus, gām, gavā, gave, gos, gavi*; du. *gāvau, gobhyām, gavos*; pl. n.v. *gāvas*, acc. *gās, gobhis, gobhyas, gavām, goṣu.*

div- f. "sky" runs: sg. n.v. *dyaus*, a. *divam, dyām*, i. *divā*, d. *dive*, ab. g. *divas*, l. *divi*; pl. n.v.a. *divas, dyubhis, dyubhyas, divām, dyuṣu.*

CONSONANTAL DECLENSION

§ 32. PRELIMINARY REMARKS. In the n. sg. masc. and fem. the ending *-s* always disappears (§ 4 I). Before an ending beginning with a vowel the final sound of the stem remains unchanged (§ 19 I); in the n. sg. and before endings beginning with consonants §§ 4 and 19 apply. It should be noted that the neuters insert a nasal in the n.a.v. pl. before the final consonant unless it is a nasal; in the stems in *s* the preceding vowel is lengthened in such a case.

§ 33. Root stems and the nouns similarly inflected (of one stem in the sg.); masc., n., and fem.

Masc. and fem. Paradigms: *vāc-* f. "voice", *marut-* m. "wind", *diś-* f. "region", *dviṣ-* m. "enemy".

Sg.

NV.	*vāk* (§ 4)	*marut* (§ 4)	*dik* (§ 4)	*dviṭ* (§ 4)
A.	*vācam*	*marutam*	*diśam*	*dviṣam*
I.	*vācā*	*marutā*	*diśā*	*dviṣā*
D.	*vāce*	*marute*	*diśe*	*dviṣe*
Ab. G.	*vācas*	*marutas*	*diśas*	*dviṣas*
L.	*vāci*	*maruti*	*diśi*	*dviṣi*

Du.

NVA.	*vācau*	*marutau*	*diśau*	*dviṣau*
IDAb.	*vāgbhyām* (§ 19)	*marudbhyām*	*digbhyām*	*dviḍbhyām*
GL.	*vācos*	*marutos*	*diśos*	*dviṣos*

Pl.

NVA.	*vācas*	*marutas*	*diśas*	*dviṣas*
I.	*vāgbhis* (§ 19)	*marudbhis*	*digbhis*	*dviḍbhis*
D. Ab.	*vāgbhyas*	*marudbhyas*	*digbhyas*	*dviḍbhyas*
G.	*vācām*	*marutām*	*diśām*	*dviṣām*
L.	*vākṣu* (§ 19)	*marutsu*	*dikṣu*	*dviṭsu*

Some additional examples: *bhiṣaj-* "doctor": *bhiṣak, bhiṣajam, bhiṣagbhis, bhiṣakṣu*; *samrāj-* "sovereign": *samrāṭ, samrājam, samrāḍbhis, samrāṭsu*; °*vṛdh-* [1] "increasing": °*vṛt,* °*vṛdham,* °*vṛdbhis,* °*vṛtsu*; °*budh-* "awakening": °*bhut,* °*budham,* °*bhudbhis,* °*bhutsu*; °*duh-* "milking": °*dhuk,* °*duham,*

[1] i.e., *vṛdh-* at the end of a compound.

°*dhugbhis,* °*dhukṣu;* °*lih-* "licking": °*liṭ,* °*liham,* °*liḍbhis,* °*liṭsu.*

The neuter *jagat-* "world" like *marut,* only n.a.v. sg. *jagat,* du. *jagatī,* pl. *jaganti.*

§ 34. STEMS IN *as is us.*

I. NEUTERS. Paradigms: *manas-* "mind", *havis-* "offering", *cakṣus-* "eye".

		Sg.	
NVA.	*manas*	*havis*	*cakṣus*
I.	*manasā*	*haviṣā* (§ 20 II)	*cakṣuṣā*
D.	*manase*	*haviṣe*	*cakṣuṣe*
Ab. G.	*manasas*	*haviṣas*	*cakṣuṣas*
L.	*manasi*	*haviṣi*	*cakṣuṣi*
		Du.	
NVA.	*manasī*	*haviṣī*	*cakṣuṣī*
IDAb.	*manobhyām* (§ 19 II)	*havirbhyām*	*cakṣurbhyām*
GL.	*manasos*	*haviṣos*	*cakṣuṣos*
		Pl.	
NVA.	*manāṃsi*	*havīṃṣi*	*cakṣūṃṣi*
I.	*manobhis* (§ 19 II)	*havirbhis* (§ 19 II; 14)	*cakṣurbhis*
D. Ab.	*manobhyas*	*havirbhyas*	*cakṣurbhyas*
G.	*manasām*	*haviṣām*	*cakṣuṣām*
L.	*manaḥsu* (or *manassu*)	*haviḥṣu* (or *haviṣṣu*)	*cakṣuḥṣu* (or *cakṣuṣṣu*)

II. MASCULINES AND FEMININES. Like the neuters (§ 34 I); only in the nom. sg. the *a* in the suffix *-as* is lengthened: *Aṅgiras-* m.: n. sg. *Aṅgirās,* a. sg. *Aṅgirasam,* i. *Aṅgirasā,* etc., n. pl. *Aṅgirasas,* etc.; *Apsaras-* f.: n. sg. *Apsarās,* a. sg. *Apsarasam,* n. pl. *Apsarasas.* Most masc. and fem. belonging here are adjectives and, in fact, compounds. Paradigms: *sumanas-* "well-disposed, cheerful", *dīrghāyus-* "long-lived".

	M. F.	N.	M. F.	N.
		Sg.		
N.	*sumanās*			
V.	*sumanas*	*sumanas* (N. V. A.)	*dīrghāyus* (N. V.)	*dīrghāyus* (N. V. A.)
A.	*sumanasam*		*dīrghāyuṣam*	
		Du.		
NVA.	*sumanasau*	*sumanasī*	*dīrghāyuṣau*	*dīrghāyuṣī*
		Pl.		
NVA.	*sumanasas*	*sumanāṃsi*	*dīrghāyuṣas*	*dīrghāyūṃṣi*

Further as above.

§ 35. Stems in *r*; here § 18, III finds application. Paradigm: *gir-* f. "speech". Sg. n.v. *gīr,* acc. *giram,* i. *girā,* etc.; du. n.a.v. *girau,* i.d.ab. *gīrbhyām,* g.l. *giros*; pl. n.a.v. *giras,* i. *gīrbhis,* d.ab. *gīrbhyas,* g. *girām,* l. *gīrṣu.* Likewise e.g., *pur-* f. "city": *pūr, puram, purā*; *purau, pūrbhyām, puros*; *puras, pūrbhis,* etc. In the n. sg. and before *bh* and *s* *āśiṣ-* "good wish, benediction" shifts to this inflection: *āsīrbhiḥ.*

§§ 36-45. Multiple-stem nouns.

Preliminary remark. The multiple-stem nouns or those with stem gradation have the strong stem with the masc. and fem. in the n.a.v. sg. and du. and in the n.v. pl., with the neuter in the n.a.v. pl. In the remaining cases the weak stem appears, but with several stem classes in a double form, depending on whether the ending begins with a consonant or with a vowel. (Exception: § 41). In the strong stem the full grade appears, in the weak stem the weak grade. — These nouns are cited in the weak stem.

§ 36. STEMS IN *at* (weak stem *at*, strong stem *ant*). These stems are almost all pres. or fut. act. participles (cf. § 101, I). Paradigm: *tudat-* "striking". (Concerning the fem., *tudatī* or also *-antī-*, see § 27).

	Sg. M.	Sg. N.	Pl. M.	Pl. N.	
NV.	*tudan*	*tudat*	*tudantas*	*tudanti*	NV.
A.	*tudantam*	*tudat*	*tudatas*	*tudanti*	A.
I.	*tudatā*		*tudadbhis*		I.
D.	*tudate*		*tudadbhyas*		D. Ab.
Ab. G.	*tudatas*		*tudatām*		G.
L.	*tudati*		*tudatsu*		L.

Du.

	M.	N.
NVA.	*tudantau*	*tudatī* (also *-antī*)
IDAb.	*tudadbhyām*	
GL.	*tudatos*	

Note. In the n.a.v du. neuter as well as in the feminine stem verbs of the 1st, 4th, 10th classes and the derivative conjugations have the strong participial stem in *ant*: *bhavantī*, *corayantī*; the verbs of the athematic conjugation (2nd, 3rd, 5th, 7th, 8th, 9th classes) have the weak stem: *dviṣatī*, *satī*, *juhvatī*, *kurvatī*; the verbs of the 6th class, the fut. part. and the pres. part. of the verbs of the 2nd class in *ā* have optionally the strong or weak stem: *tudatī*: *tudantī*; *dāsyatī*: *dāsyantī* (fut. part. *dā-* "give"), *yātī*: *yāntī* (from *yā-* 2nd class "go").

§ 37. Reduplicated stems form all cases (except n.a.v. pl. n., where the strong form also occurs) from the weak stem. Paradigm: *dadat-* "giving" (part. of *dā-*, 3rd or reduplicating class). Sg. m. n.v. *dadat*, acc. *dadatam*, i. *dadatā*, etc., n. n.a.v. *dadat*; du. m. n.a.v. *dadatau*, n. *dadatī*; pl. m. n.a.v. *dadatas*, n. n.a.v. *dadati* (or *dadanti*).

The word *mahat-* "great" has the strong stem *mahānt-*. Thus: sg. m. n. *mahān*, acc. *mahāntam*, i. *mahatā*, etc.; n. n.a.v. *mahat*; du. m. n.a.v. *mahāntau*, n. *mahatī*; pl. m. n.v. *mahāntas*, acc. *mahatas*, n. n.a.v. *mahānti*. Continues like *tudat-*.

§ 38. Stems in *vat* and *mat*. Possessive adjectives. They are inflected just like the participles in *at* (§ 36), but form the n. sg. m. in *vān* and *mān*, thus from *balavat-* "strong" (*bala-* "strength"): *balavān*, v. *balavan*, *balavantam*, *balavatā*, etc., du. *balavantau*, pl. n. *balavantas*, acc. *balavatas*, etc.; from *dhīmat-* "intelligent" (*dhī-* "thought"): *dhīmān*, *dhīman*, *dhīmantam*, *dhīmatā*, etc.; from *kṛtavat-* "having done" (§ 103): *kṛtavān*, etc. — *bhavat-* as a polite pronoun of the 2nd person (with the 3rd person of the verb) is inflected likewise: *bhavān*, *bhavantam*, *bhavatā*.

§ 39. Stems in *an*, *man*, *van*. Almost only masc. and neuters; a fem. like *sīman-* "boundary", and an adj. m. like *pīvan-* (f. *pīvarī-*) "fat" are declined like *rājan-* (only *pīvan-* n. sg. m. also *pīvān*). The stems formed with *man* and *van* have *an*, not *n* in the weak forms before vocalic ending if a consonant precedes the *m* or *v*. Paradigms: *rājan-* m. "king", *nāman-* n. "name", *ātman-* m. "soul, self".

		Sg.	
N.	*rājā*	*nāma*	*ātmā*
V.	*rājan*	*nāma*	*ātman*
A.	*rājānam*	*nāma*	*ātmānam*
I.	*rājñā*	*nāmnā*	*ātmanā*
D.	*rājñe*	*nāmne*	*ātmane*
Ab. G.	*rājñas*	*nāmnas*	*ātmanas*
L.	*rājñi, rājani*	*nāmni, nāmani*	*ātmani*
		Du.	
NVA.	*rājānau*	*nāmnī, nāmanī*	*ātmānau*
IDAb.	*rājabhyām*	*nāmabhyām*	*ātmabhyām*
G.L.	*rājños*	*nāmnos*	*ātmanos*
		Pl.	
NV.	*rājānas*	*nāmāni*	*ātmānas*
A.	*rājñas*	*nāmāni*	*ātmanas*
I.	*rājabhis*	*nāmabhis*	*ātmabhis*
DAb.	*rājabhyas*	*nāmabhyas*	*ātmabhyas*
G.	*rājñām*	*nāmnām*	*ātmanām*
L.	*rājasu*	*nāmasu*	*ātmasu*

The word *brahman-* n. "fundamental principle, Brahman" runs thus: *brahma, brahmaṇā* (§ 20 I), *brahmaṇe,* etc.

Note. voc. sg. n. is also *nāman.*

§ 40. The word *śvan-* m. "dog" is inflected: *śvā, śvan, śvānam, śunā, śune, śunas, śuni*; *śvānau, śvabhyām, śunos*; pl. n.v. *śvānas,* acc. *śunas, śvabhis, śvabhyas, śunām, śvasu*; *yuvan-* adj. and m. "young, youth": *yuvā, yuvan, yuvānam, yūnā, yūne,* etc.; *yuvānau, yuvabhyām, yūnos*; *yuvānas, yūnas, yuvabhis,* etc.

§ 41. Stems in *in*; mostly possessive adjectives. Paradigm: *balin-* "having power (*bala-*), powerful". Concerning the fem. (*balinī-*) see § 27.

	Sg. M.	Sg. N.	Du. M.	Du. N.	Pl. M.	Pl. N.
N.	*balī*	*bali*				
V.	*balin*	*bali(n)*	*balinau*	*balinī*	*balinas*	*balīni*
A.	*balinam*	*bali*				
I.	*balinā*				*balibhis*	
D.	*baline*		*balibhyām*		*balibhyas*	
Ab.	*balinas*					
G.			*balinos*		*balinām*	
L.	*balini*				*baliṣu*	

§ 42. The perfect participles in *vas*. Paradigm: *vidvas-* "knowing". Concerning the fem. (*viduṣī-*) see § 27.

	Sg. M.	Sg. N.	Du. M.	Du. N.	Pl. M.	Pl. N.
N.	*vidvān*				*vidvāṃsas*	
V.	*vidvan*	*vidvat*	*vidvāṃsau*	*viduṣī*		*vidvāṃsi*
A.	*vidvāṃsam*				*viduṣas*	
I.	*viduṣā*				*vidvadbhis*	
D.	*viduṣe*		*vidvadbhyām*		*vidvadbhyas*	
Ab.	*viduṣas*					
G.			*viduṣos*		*viduṣām*	
L.	*viduṣi*				*vidvatsu*	

§ 43. THE COMPARATIVES IN (*ī*)*yas*. Paradigms: *śreyas-* "better"; *garīyas-* "heavier". Concerning the fem. (*śreyasī-*, *garīyasī-*), see § 27.

	M.	N.	M.	N.
		Sg.		
N.	*śreyān*	*śreyas*	*garīyān*	*garīyas*
V.	*śreyan*		*garīyan*	
A.	*śreyāṃsam*		*garīyāṃsam*	
I.	*śreyasā*, etc. (like § 34)		*garīyasā*, etc.	
		Du.		
NVA.	*śreyāṃsau*	*śreyasī*	*garīyāṃsau*	*garīyasī*
I.	*śreyobhyām*, etc.		*garīyobhyām*, etc.	
		Pl.		
NV.	*śreyāṃsas*	*śreyāṃsi*	*garīyāṃsas*	*garīyāṃsi*
A.	*śreyasas*		*garīyasas*	
I.	*śreyobhis*, etc.		*garīyobhis*, etc.	

§ 44. THE ADJECTIVES IN *ac*. They are originally compounds of the root *ac-* (strong form *añc-*) "turn, go" with prepositions and with some other words. There are two types: *prāc-* "easterly" (really "turned forwards") and *pratyac-* "westerly" (really "turned backwards, situated behind"). The fem. is also formed here by addition of *ī* to the weak stem (in prevocalic form): *prācī*, *pratīcī-* (§ 27). Like *prāc-* run e.g., *apāc-* "situated backward, behind", *avāc-* "directed downwards", *parāc-* "turned away", *arvāc-* "coming hither"; like *pratyac-* e.g., *nyac-* "directed downwards", *samyac-* "united, common", *udac-* "directed upward, northerly"; fem. *apācī-*, etc., *nīcī-*, *udīcī-*.

	M.	N.	M.	N.
		Sg.		
NV.	*prāṅ* (§ 4 IV)	*prāk*	*pratyaṅ*	*pratyak*
A.	*prāñcam*		*pratyañcam*	
I.		*prācā*		*pratīcā*
D.		*prāce*		*pratīce*
Ab. G.		*prācas*		*pratīcas*
L.		*prāci*		*pratīci*
		Du.		
NVA	*prāñcau*	*prācī*	*pratyañcau*	*pratīcī*
IDAb.		*prāgbhyām* (§§ 19; 10)		*pratyagbhyām*
G.L.		*prācos*		*pratīcos*
		Pl.		
NV.	*prāñcas*	*prāñci*	*pratyañcas*	*pratyañci*
A.	*prācas*		*pratīcas*	
I.		*prāgbhis*		*pratyagbhis*
D. Ab.		*prāgbhyas*		*pratyagbhyas*
G.		*prācām*		*pratīcām*
L.		*prākṣu* (§§ 19 II; 4 IV)		*pratyakṣu*

The word *tiryac-* "horizontal" has *tiraśc-* in the prevocalic form of the weak stem, thus *tiryaṅ, tiryañcam, tiraścā,* etc., fem. *tiraścī-*; *viṣvac-* "going asunder, turned in both directions" runs *viṣvaṅ, viṣvañcam, viṣūcā,* etc., fem. *viṣūcī-*.

§ 45. Stems containing peculiarities.

I. The word *ahan-* n. "day" is inflected: sg. n.v.a. *ahar* (*ahaḥ*, § 4 VI), i. *ahnā*, d. *ahne*, ab. g. *ahnas*, l. *ahni*, *ahani*; du. n.v.a. *ahnī*, *ahanī*, i.d.ab. *ahobhyām*, g.l. *ahnos*; pl. n.v.a. *ahāni*, i. *ahobhis*, d.ab. *ahobhyas*, g. *ahnām*, l. *ahaḥsu*, *ahassu*.

II. The neuters *akṣan-* "eye", *asthan-* "bone", *dadhan-*

"sour milk", and *sakthan-* "thigh" form only the weak prevocalic forms of the stem: *akṣṇā, akṣṇe, akṣṇas,* etc., *asthnā,* etc., *dadhnā,* etc., *sakthnā,* g. *sakthnas,* du. *sakthnī, sakthnos*; the remaining cases are formed from the *i*-stems *akṣi-, asthi-, dadhi-, sakthi-,* thus: *akṣi, akṣibhyām, asthibhis, dadhi, sakthibhyām,* etc.

III. The word *path-* "way" runs: sg. n.v. *panthās,* a. *panthānam,* i. *pathā,* l. *pathi,* etc.; du. *panthānau, pathibhyām, pathos*; pl. *panthānas, pathas, pathibhis, pathām,* etc.

IV. *puṃs-* m. "man": sg. *pumān, puman, pumāṃsam, puṃsā,* etc.; du. *pumāṃsau, pumbhyām* (*puṃbhyām,* § 12 III), *puṃsos*; pl. *pumāṃsas, puṃsas, pumbhis* (*puṃbhis*), *puṃsām,* etc.

V. *ap-* f. "water" occurs only in the plur.: n.v. *āpas,* a. *apas, adbhis, adbhyas, apām, apsu.*

VI. At the end of compounds °*han-* "killing" has the strong stem °*han*: n. sg. °*hā,* n.v.a. pl. °*hāni,* the weak prevocalic stem °*ghn-,* thus i. sg. of *brahmahan-* "murderer of Brahmans": *brahmaghnā* beside acc. sg. *brahmahaṇam,* i. pl. *brahmahabhis* (§ 39).

COMPARISON

§ 46. Comparative and superlative can be formed in a twofold way. In the first place, the comp. is formed by addition of *tara,* the sup. by addition of *tama* to the masculine stem of the adjective: *puṇya-* "pure": *puṇyatara-* "purer", *puṇyatama-* "purest"; *balin-* (§ 41): *balitara-, balitama-*; *vidvas-* (§ 42): *vidvattara-, vidvattama-.* Adjectives with a twofold stem thus have the weak preconsonantal form. The inflection is as above (§ 22).

Secondly, with a number of adjectives *īyas* is joined in the comp., *iṣṭha* in the sup. (inflection like §§ 21; 22) to the root underlying the adj. which is usually a guṇa (full grade) formation; the suffix characteristic of the positive of the adj. is thus lacking to the comp. and sup. Examples: *kṣud-ra-* "small" (root *kṣud-* "trample"): c. *kṣodīyas-*, s. *kṣodiṣṭha-*; *lagh-u-* "light": *laghīyas-*, *laghiṣṭha-*; *gur-u-* "heavy": *garīyas-*, *gariṣṭha-*; *pṛth-u-* "wide" (root *prath-* "extend"): *prathīyas-*, *prathiṣṭha-*; *dū-ra-* "far": *davīyas-*, *daviṣṭha-*; *bhū-ri-* "abundant, much, numerous" (root *bhū-* "grow"): *bhūyas-* "more", *bhūyiṣṭha-*. Sometimes the positive of the same root is lacking: (*alpa-* "small":) *kanīyas-* "smaller, younger", *kaniṣṭha-*; *śreyas-* "better", *śreṣṭha-* "best"; *jyāyas-* "older", *jyeṣṭha-*, "oldest".

Note. Occasionally forms like *śreṣṭhatara-*, *śreṣṭhatama-* with both suffixes are found.

PRONOUNS

PRELIMINARY REMARK. The paradigms of the pronominal inflection have generally originated from the union of several stems. They lack the vocative.

§ 47. PERSONAL PRONOUNS. Preliminary remarks. Singular, dual, and plural are of different stems; natural gender is not designated; in addition to several stressed forms are found enclitic forms [1]). The forms for the 1st person sg. *mad-*, pl. *asmad-*, for the 2nd person sg. *tvad-*, pl. *yuṣmad-*, appearing in the first member of a compound are used as stems; *mad-gṛha-* "my house".

---

[1]) These are enclosed in parentheses in the paradigms.

First person "I, we two, we".

	Sg.	Du.	Pl.
N.	*aham*	*āvām*	*vayam*
A.	*mām* (*mā*)	*āvām* (*nau*)	*asmān* (*nas*)
I.	*mayā*	*āvābhyām*	*asmābhis*
D.	*mahyam* (*me*)	*āvābhyām* (*nau*)	*asmabhyam* (*nas*)
Ab.	*mat*	*āvābhyām*	*asmat*
G.	*mama* (*me*)	*āvayos* (*nau*)	*asmākam* (*nas*)
L.	*mayi*	*āvayos*	*asmāsu*

Second person "you, you two, you (pl.)".

	Sg.	Du.	Pl.
N.	*tvam*	*yuvām*	*yūyam*
A.	*tvām* (*tvā*)	*yuvām* (*vām*)	*yuṣmān* (*vas*)
I.	*tvayā*	*yuvābhyām*	*yuṣmābhis*
D.	*tubhyam* (*te*)	*yuvābhyām* (*vām*)	*yuṣmabhyam* (*vas*)
Ab.	*tvat*	*yuvābhyām*	*yuṣmat*
G.	*tava* (*te*)	*yuvayos* (*vām*)	*yuṣmākam* (*vas*)
L.	*tvayi*	*yuvayos*	*yuṣmāsu*

Note 1. The ablatives can also be expressed *mattas*, *tvattas*, etc.

Note 2. The infrequent possessive pronouns are: *madīya-* or *māmaka-* "my", *tvadīya-* (*tāvaka-*) "your"; *asmadīya-* "our", *yuṣmadīya-* "your (pl.)"; *bhavadīya-* "your" (polite); *sva-*, *svaka-*, *svakīya-* "one's own, his, her", etc.

§§ 48-50. THE REMAINING, SO-CALLED "GENDER-BEARING" PRONOUNS. Preliminary remarks. The form of the n. sg. neutr. is used as stem in §§ 48-50; the latter also appears at the beginning of a compound. The endings deviating repeatedly from those of the nouns should be noted. The adverbs in *-tra* which designate place are also used instead of a locative: *tatra vane* = *tasmin vane* "in that forest".

§§ 48-49. DEMONSTRATIVE PRONOUNS.

§ 48. The stem *tad-* is also used instead of a personal pronoun of the third person "he, she, it".

Paradigm:

	Sg. M.	Sg. N.	Sg. F.	Du. M.	Du. N.	Du. F.	Pl. M.	Pl. N.	Pl. F.
N.	*sas*	*tat*	*sā*	*tau*	*te*	*te*	*te*	*tāni*	*tās*
A.	*tam*		*tām*				*tān*		
I.	*tena*		*tayā*	*tābhyām*			*tais*		*tābhis*
D.	*tasmai*		*tasyai*				*tebhyas*		*tābhyas*
Ab.	*tasmāt*		*tasyās*						
G.	*tasya*			*tayos*			*teṣām*		*tāsām*
L.	*tasmin*		*tasyām*				*teṣu*		*tāsu*

Likewise *etad-* "this": n. sg. *eṣas,* f. *eṣā,* n. *etat.* The forms *saḥ, eṣaḥ* occur only in absolute final position and before vowels, before which § 15 is applied. Within the sentence *sa, eṣa* appear before consonants.

The stem *enad-* "he" (enclit.) occurs only in the acc. of the three numbers, in the i. sg. and g. l. du. The inflection is like that of the stem *tad-*, thus *enam, enat, enām, enena,* etc.

§ 49. Stem *idam-* "this".

	Sg. M.	Sg. F.	Du. M.	Du. F.	Pl. M.	Pl. F.
N.	*ayam*	*iyam*	*imau*	*ime*	*ime*	*imās*
A.	*imam*	*imām*			*imān*	
I.	*anena*	*anayā*	*ābhyām*		*ebhis*	*ābhis*
D.	*asmai*	*asyai*			*ebhyas*	*ābhyas*
Ab.	*asmāt*	*asyās*				
G.	*asya*		*anayos*		*eṣām*	*āsām*
L.	*asmin*	*asyām*			*eṣu*	*āsu*

Neutr. n. a. sg. *idam*, du. *ime*, pl. *imāni*. Otherwise like masc.

Stem *adas-* "that".

	Sg. M.	Sg. F.	Du. M.N.F.	Pl. M.	Pl. F.
N.	*asau*	*asau*	*amū*	*amī*	*amūs*
A.	*amum*	*amūm*		*amūn*	
I.	*amunā*	*amuyā*	*amūbhyām*	*amībhis*	*amūbhis*
D.	*amuṣmai*	*amuṣyai*		*amībhyas*	*amūbhyas*
Ab.	*amuṣmāt*	*amuṣyās*			
G.	*amuṣya*		*amuyos*	*amīṣām*	*amūṣām*
L.	*amuṣmin*	*amuṣyām*		*amīṣu*	*amūṣu*

Neutr. n. a. sg. *adas*, pl. *amūni*. Otherwise like masc.

§ 50. Relative pronoun. The stem is *yad-* "which"; it is declined like *tad-*. Thus sg. n. m. *yas*, n. *yat*, f. *yā*, acc. *yam*, *yat*, *yām*; du. n. a. m. *yau*, n. *ye*, f. *ye*; pl. n.m. *ye*, n. *yāni*, f. *yās*, acc. *yān*, *yāni*, *yās*, etc.

Interrogative pronoun. Stem *kim*, declensional stem *ka-*. This pronoun, apart from the n. and a. sg. n. (*kim*), is declined like *tad-*. Thus: sg. n. m. *kas*, n. *kim*, f. *kā*, acc. *kam*, *kim*, *kām*; du. n. a. m. *kau*, n. *ke*, f. *ke*; pl. n.m. *ke*, n. *kāni*, f. *kās*, acc. *kān*, *kāni*, *kās*, etc. Indefinites are formed by addition of *api*, *cid*, *cana* to the interrogative pronoun, e.g., *kaḥ* "who?": *ko 'pi*, *kaścit*, *kaścana* "anyone"; *kva* "where?" *kvāpi*, etc. "anywhere"; *kim api* "anything at all", *na kiṃcid* "nothing", etc.

§ 51. Pronominals (pronominally inflected adjectives).

1. A number of adjectives are declined like *yad-* (§ 50): *katara-* "which of two?", *katama-* "which (of several)", *itara-* "other", *anya-* "other", etc.

II. The words *sarva-* and *viśva-* "all, every", *eka-* "one", *ekatara-* "one of two" are likewise declined pronominally, only in the n. acc. sg. n. they have the adjectival ending: *viśvam, ekam.*

III. Other words are treated like *sarva-*, etc., but can also be declined according to the nominal declension in the ab. l. sg. m. n. and in the n. pl. m.: *adhara-* "situated below, lower", *antara-* "inner", *apara-* "other", *avara-* "posterior, western", *uttara-* "situated above, northern", *dakṣiṇa-* "to the right, southern", *para-* "later, other", *paścima-* "western", *pūrva-* "earlier", *sva-* "one's own". — Also *ubhaya-* "both kinds", which has *ubhayī-* in the fem.

§ 52. Nouns used instead of pronouns. It is worth noting that *ātman-* "soul, self" is used instead of a reflexive pronoun: *Vāsavadattā . . . ātmānam Udayanāya prāyacchat* "V . . . gave herself to U."; it represents all three persons, and the sg. is also used when the word refers to a du. or pl.

sva- serves for all persons as a reflexive with a predominantly possessive meaning; thus it is usually to be translated by "one's own" or Lat. *suus*. The designation of the refl. is, however, not obligatory.

In polite address *bhavat-* (n. sg. m. *bhavān*, f. *bhavatī*, n. pl. m. *bhavantas*, etc., § 38) is used as a pronoun of the 2nd person (with the 3rd person of the verb).

NUMERALS

§ 53. Cardinals.

1 *eka-*, 2 *dvi-*, 3 *tri-*, 4 *catur-*, 5 *pañca-*, 6 *ṣaṣ-*, 7 *sapta-*, 8 *aṣṭa-*, 9 *nava-*, 10 *daśa-*, 11 *ekādaśa-*, 12 *dvādaśa-*, 13 *trayo-*

daśa-, 14 *caturdaśa-*, 15 *pañcadaśa-*, 16 *ṣoḍaśa-*, 17 *saptadaśa-*, 18 *aṣṭādaśa-*, 19 *navadaśa-*, *ekonaviṃśati-* or *ūnaviṃśati-*, 20 *viṃśati-*, 21 *ekaviṃśati-*, 22 *dvāviṃśati-*, 23 *trayoviṃśati-*, 24 *caturv.*, 26 *ṣaḍv.*, 28 *aṣṭāv.*, 29 *navav.* or *ūnatriṃśat-*, 30 *triṃśat-*, 31 *ekatriṃśat-*, 32 *dvāt.*, 33 *trayast.*, 40 *catvāriṃśat-*, 50 *pañcāśat-*, 60 *ṣaṣṭi-*, 62 *dvāṣaṣṭi-* or *dviṣ.*, 63 *trayaḥṣ.* or *triṣ.*, 70 *saptati-*, 80 *aśīti-*, 81 *ekāśīti-*, 82 *dvyaśīti-*, 88 *aṣṭāśīti-*, 90 *navati-*, 100 *śata-*, 200 *dve śate* or *dviśata-*, 300 *trīṇi śatāni* or *triśata-*, 1000 *sahasra-*, 10,000 *ayuta-*, 100,000 *lakṣa-*, 1,000,000 *prayuta-*, 10,000,000 *koṭi-*.

The numbers 2, 3, 8 with 20 and 30 run *dvā*, *trayas*, *aṣṭā*, with 80 *dvi*, *tri*, *aṣṭa*, with 40-70, 90 both forms occur.

The cardinal numbers between the hundreds are usually expressed with addition of *adhika-* "more": 101 *ekādhikaṃ śatam*, 105 *pañcādhikaṃ śatam* (or *pañcādhikaśatam*).

§ 54. Declension of the cardinal numbers. *eka-* 1 is inflected according to § 51 II, the pl. *eke* means "some"; in epic and in later literature the sg. is also encountered with the meaning "a certain, a". *dvi-* 2 is inflected as a dual of *dva-* (thus §§ 21; 22): m. *dvau*, n. *dve*, f. *dve*, etc., *tri-* and *catur-* as follows:

	M.	N.	F.	M.	N.	F.
NV.	*trayas*	*trīṇi*	*tisras*	*catvāras*	*catvāri*	*catasras*
A.	*trīn*	*trīṇi*	*tisras*	*caturas*	*catvāri*	*catasras*
I.	*tribhis*		*tisṛbhis*	*caturbhis*		*catasṛbhis*
DAb.	*tribhyas*		*tisṛbhyas*	*caturbhyas*		*catasṛbhyas*
G.	*trayāṇām*		*tisṛṇām*	*caturṇām*		*catasṛṇām*
L.	*triṣu*		*tisṛṣu*	*caturṣu*		*catasṛṣu*

The numerals 5, 7, 8, 9, 10, and 11-19 are inflected for all genders: n.a.v. *pañca*, i. *pañcabhis*, d.ab. *pañcabhyas*, g.

pañcānām, l. *pañcasu*; only 8 runs also: *aṣṭau, aṣṭābhis, aṣṭābhyas, aṣṭāsu*; 6: *ṣaṭ, ṣaḍbhis, ṣaḍbhyas, ṣaṇṇām, ṣaṭsu.* The numbers 1-19 are usually used adjectivally: *pañcabhir vīraiḥ* "with 5 men".

The numbers 20 to 99 are feminine substantives in the sg.; 100, 1000, etc. are neuter subst. in the sg.; they have the numbered things either as appositives in the same case of the plur. or in the gen. plur.; they can also be joined with them in a compound: *viṃśatir aśvāḥ, viṃśatir aśvānām* "20 horses", *viṃśatyā vīrais* or *vīrāṇām* "with 20 men", *varṣaśatam* "100 years".

§ 55. Ordinals.

1st *prathama-* (f. *-mā*), 2nd *dvitīya-*, 3rd *tṛtīya-*, 4th *caturtha-* (f. *-thī*) or *turīya-* (f. *-yā*), 5th *pañcama-* (f. *-mī*), 6th *ṣaṣṭha-*, 7th *saptama-*, 8th *aṣṭama-*, 9th *navama-*, 10th *daśama-*, 11th *ekādaśa-*, 12th *dvādaśa-*, 20th *viṃśatitama-* (f. *-ī*) or *viṃśa-* (f. *-ī*), *triṃśattama-* or *triṃśa-*, 40th *catvāriṃśattama-* or *catvāriṃśa-*, 50th *pañcāśattama-* or *pañcāśa-*, 60th only *ṣaṣṭitama-*, but 61st *ekaṣaṣṭitama-* or *ekaṣaṣṭa-*, etc.

§ 56. Numeral adverbs. Numeral adverbs are *sakṛt* 1 ×, *dviḥ* 2 ×, *triḥ* 3 ×, *catuḥ* 4 ×, *pañcakṛtvaḥ* 5 ×, etc. The adverbs in *-dhā*: *ekadhā*, etc. form expressions for "singly, at one time, etc.", those in *-śas*: *pañcaśas*, etc. for "in fives, etc.", *ekaśas* "individually".

CONJUGATION

§ 57. PRELIMINARY REMARKS.

I. There are three voices in Sanskrit, the active (parasmaipadam), the middle (ātmanepadam), and the passive. Some verbs occur only in the active (e.g., *asti* "be"), some only in the middle (e.g., *āste* "sit"). Of the passive almost only a present exists; in the non-present forms the middle is also used with passive meaning. The middle in general expresses actions which the agent carries out "for himself, in his own interest": *yajati* "he sacrifices (for another)": *yajate* "he sacrifices (for himself)". This original distinction is frequently preserved in Vedic and is not completely lost in classical Sanskrit either: we often find a quite significant use of the middle; yet the forms of these two types are used promiscuously, e.g., for metrical reasons or even optionally.

II. The moods are: indicative, optative, imperative; only the present has three moods, the remaining tenses only the indicative; the infrequent precative is, however, a kind of aorist optative.
The tenses are: present and imperfect, which form the present system with opt. and pres. imp., future, the rare conditional, aorist, perfect. The three latter groups are called the general forms of the verb; they, as also the passive, are formed from the root: the verbs of the *aya*-class, however, form fut. and perf. from the present stem. The whole present system is formed from the so-called present stem.

III. Sanskrit distinguishes also with respect to the verb: singular, dual (the number two: we two, etc.), and plural.

IV. The personal endings are of two kinds: primary (in the pres., fut. indic.) and secondary (in the imperf., aor., opt., and condit.), disregarding the endings deviating in several persons of the imperative and perfect.

The primary endings are in general:

In the active: sing. 1st *-mi*, 2nd *-si*, 3rd *-ti*; du. 1st *-vas*, 2nd *-thas*, 3rd *-tas*; pl. 1st *-mas*, 2nd *-tha*, 3rd *-anti* (*-nti*);

in the middle: *-e*, *-se*, *-te*; *-vahe*, *-āthe*, *-āte*; *-mahe*, *-dhve*, *-ate* (*-nte*).

The secondary endings are:

in the active: *-am* (*-m*), *-s*, *-t*; *-va*, *-tam*, *-tām*; *-ma*, *-ta*, *-an* (*-n*);

in the middle: *-i*, *-thās*, *-ta*; *-vahi*, *-āthām*, *-ātām*; *-mahi*, *-dhvam*, *-ata* (*-nta*).

The optative has in the 1st sg. act. the ending *-m* or *-am*; mid. *-a*, in the 2nd du. mid. *-āthām*, 3rd du. mid. *-ātām*, in the 3rd pl. act. *-ur*, mid. *-ran*.

The endings of the imperative are:

in the active: *-āni*, *-dhi* or without ending, *-tu*; *-āva*, *-tam*, *-tām*; *-āma*, *-ta*, *-antu* (*-ntu*);

in the middle: *-ai*, *-sva*, *-tām*; *-āvahai*, *-āthām*, *-ātām*; *-āmahai*, *-dhvam*, *-antām* (*-ntām*).

The endings of the perfect are given in § 84. Cf. also the paradigms.

V. In the impf., aor., and condit. the augment, i.e., an *a-* placed before the verbal stem, appears: *tudati* "he pushes": *a-tudat* "he pushed". Roots beginning with vowels have vṛddhi instead of this *a*: *asyati* "he throws": impf. *āsyat*: *ukṣati* "he wets": impf. *aukṣat*. In the case of roots compounded with prepositions the augment appears between prep. and verb: *nir-a-gacchat*, 3rd sg. impf. of *niḥ* + *gacchati*. In epic Skr. the augment is sometimes lacking: *uddharam* (§ 17) = *udaharam* (1st sg. impf. act., root *hṛ-*, *harati* "take"); *pravartata* = *prāvartata* (*pra* + *avartata*, 3rd sg. impf. mid. root *vṛt-* + *pra* "arise"). Aorist forms without augment are used after the prohibitive *mā*: *mā gās* ("do not go", *gās* 2nd sg. aor. act. without augment, root *gā-* "go"), cf. § 82.

VI. RULES FOR REDUPLICATION. There are a number of reduplicated verbal forms. The reduplication consists in the fact that a part of the root, as a rule the first consonant with a vowel, is prefixed to the root, e.g., *pu-puṣ-*: *puṣ-* "flourish". The following rules apply:

1. The aspirates are reduplicated by the corresponding non-aspirates: *bhī-*: *bi-bhī-*; *dhāv-*: *da-dhāv-*.

2. Velars are reduplicated by the corresponding palatals: *khan-*: *cakhan-*; *gṛ-*: *jāgar-*; *h* is reduplicated by *j*: *hu-*: *juhu-*.

3. Of two initial consonants only the first is reduplicated: *svap-*: *suṣvap-* (§ 20 II), *tvar-*: *tatvar-*, *śru-*: *śuśru-*. Roots which begin with velar + cons. form the reduplication syllable with the corresponding palatal here also: *kram-*: *cakram-*, *grah-*: *jagrah-*, *hrī-*: *jihrī-*. But if the first of the initial consonants is a sibilant and the second is voiceless, the latter or its representative is reduplicated: *sthā-*: *tiṣṭha-*, *skand-*: *caskand-*; but *smṛ-*: *sasmar-*.

The vowel of the reduplication syllable is given with the respective paradigms.

PRESENT STEMS

§ 58. The present of Sanskrit is divided into ten classes according to the structure of the present stem. These classes are divided into two groups, into the thematic and the athematic conjugation. In the thematic conj. the present stem ends in *a* and always remains constant. In the athematic conjugation the stem is variable: it has strong and weak forms. The 1st, 4th, 6th, 10th classes belong to the thematic conjugation, the 2nd, 3rd, 5th, 7th, 8th, 9th classes belong to the athematic conjugation. This enumeration, which follows the native grammar, is a well-established one which should not be changed arbitrarily. These class distinctions relate only to the present, act. and mid., not to the remaining tenses (concerning the passive and the derived conjugations, s. §§ 95 ff.). In several cases two or more than two presents have existed for one root.

THEMATIC CONJUGATION

§ 59. Common to the four thematic present classes are:

1. The stem ends in *a* (s. § 58). This *a* becomes *ā* before the endings beginning with *m* and *v* and coalesces with the middle ending *e*. The dual endings of the mid. are *-et(h)e*, *-et(h)ām*.

2. The 2nd sg. imperat. act. is identical to the stem.

3. The optative suffix is *ī*, before vowels *īy*, which contracts with the *a* of the stem to *e* (*ey*). The ending of the 1st sg. act. is *-am* in the opt.

The inflection is the same in the four classes. Only the formation of the stem is different.

In the 1st class *a* is added to the strong (guṇated) root: *bhū-*: *bhav-ati* [1]), *bhṛ-*: *bhar-ati*, *ruh-*: *roh-ati*, *ji-*: *jay-ati*, *nī-*: *nay-ati*, *pat-*: *pat-ati*. Exceptions are (s. § 3): *nind-*: *nind-ati*, *krīḍ-*: *krīḍ-ati*.

In the 6th class *a* is added to the weak root: *tud-*: *tud-ati*, *viś-*: *viś-ati*. Final *ṝ* of the root becomes *ir* before the thematic vowel (before the *a*): *tṝ-*: *tir-ati*. To the root *prach-* belongs the present *pṛcchati* (sic!; 61 I).

In the 4th class *ya* is added to the unchanged root: *paś-*: *paś-yati*, *as-*: *as-yati*.

In the 10th class and with the causatives *aya* is added to the root: *dūṣ-*: *dūṣ-ayati*, *bhū-*: *bhāv-ayati*; *tuṣ-*: *toṣayati*. Further §§ 97.98.

§ 60. First Class. Paradigm: *bhṛ-* "bear".

	Sg.	Du.	Pl.
		Indicative	
		Act.	
1st	*bharāmi*	*bharāvas*	*bharāmas*
2nd	*bharasi*	*bharathas*	*bharatha*
3rd	*bharati*	*bharatas*	*bharanti*
		Mid.	
1st	*bhare*	*bharāvahe*	*bharāmahe*
2nd	*bharase*	*bharethe*	*bharadhve*
3rd	*bharate*	*bharete*	*bharante*

[1]) The verbs are usually cited either by the root or by the 3rd sing. pres. act. ind.

	Sg.	Du.	Pl.
		Imperfect	
		Act.	
1st	*abharam*	*abharāva*	*abharāma*
2nd	*abharas*	*abharatam*	*abharata*
3rd	*abharat*	*abharatām*	*abharan*
		Mid.	
1st	*abhare*	*abharāvahi*	*abharāmahi*
2nd	*abharathās*	*abharethām*	*abharadhvam*
3rd	*abharata*	*abharetām*	*abharanta*
		Optative	
		Act.	
1st	*bhareyam*	*bhareva*	*bharema*
2nd	*bhares*	*bharetam*	*bhareta*
3rd	*bharet*	*bharetām*	*bhareyur*
		Mid.	
1st	*bhareya*	*bharevahi*	*bharemahi*
2nd	*bharethās*	*bhareyāthām*	*bharedhvam*
3rd	*bhareta*	*bhareyātām*	*bhareran*
		Imperative	
		Act.	
1st	*bharāṇi* (§ 20 I)	*bharāva*	*bharāma*
2nd	*bhara*	*bharatam*	*bharata*
3rd	*bharatu*	*bharatām*	*bharantu*
		Mid.	
1st	*bharai*	*bharāvahai*	*bharāmahai*
2nd	*bharasva*	*bharethām*	*bharadhvam*
3rd	*bharatām*	*bharetām*	*bharantām*

In the same way: *tud-* "push": *tudati* VI, *as-* "throw": *asyati* IV, etc.

§ 61. I. Some verbs of the thematic classes form the present stem with the suffix *ccha*: *gam-* "go": pres. *gacchati* I, *yam-* "stretch": *yacchati* I, *iṣ-* "wish": *icchati* VI, *vas-* "become bright": *ucchati* VI, *ṛ-* "go": *ṛcchati* VI. To the root *prach-* "ask": *pṛcchati* VI.

II. Some roots have the long vowel: *tam-* "be benumbed": *tāmyati*, *dam-* "tame": *dāmyati*, *bhram-* "wander": *bhrāmyati*, *mad-* "be excited, rejoice": *mādyati*, *śam-* "become quiet": *śāmyati*, *śram-* "become tired": *śrāmyati*, *div-* "play, throw dice": *dīvyati*, *guh-* "hide": *gūhati*; *ā-cam-* "sip" has usually *ācāmati*; *kram-* "step" forms in the act. *krāmati*, in the middle *kramate*.
The root *jan-* "be born" has the present *jāyate* IV.

III. Some roots which have a penultimate nasal lose this: *daṃś-* "bite": *daśati* I, *sañj-* "hang": *sajati* I, *bhraṃś-* "fall": *bhraśyate*, *bhraśyati* IV, *rañj-* "redden": *rajyati* IV; *svañj-* "embrace": *svajate*, *svajati*.

IV. A number of roots insert a nasal before the final consonant of the root: *kṛt-* "cut": *kṛntati* VI, *lip-* "besmear": *limpati* VI, *lup-* "break in pieces": *lumpati* VI, *muc-* "let loose": *muñcati* VI, *sic-* "sprinkle": *siñcati* VI, *vid-* "find": *vindati* VI.

V. Some roots are reduplicated; *sthā-* "stand": *tiṣṭhati* I, *ghrā-* "smell": *jighrati* I, with dissimilation: *pā-* "drink": *pibati* I, with loss of the *s* and lengthening of the vowel: *sad-* "sit": *sīdati* (**si-sda-ti*).

VI. The root *vyadh-* "bore through" forms the present *vidhyati*; *śā-* "whet": *śyati* (IV), *ava-sā-* "unyoke, etc.": °*syati*.

VII. For *dṛś-* "see" *paśyati* is substituted as a present.

The 10th class will be discussed in § 98.

ATHEMATIC CONJUGATION

§ 62. General preliminary remarks. 1. Stem gradation exists in all classes. The strong form of the stem is found in 13 persons, namely:

1. in the three persons of the sing. indic. active;
2. in the three persons of the sing. impf. active;
3. in all first persons of the imper. active and middle;
4. in the third person sing. of the imper. active.

2. It should be noted that some personal endings differ from those of the thematic conj.; cf. the paradigms. The 2nd sg. imper. act. has the ending *-dhi*, after a vowel *-hi*.

3. As an optative suffix *-yā-* (before *-ur* of the 3rd pl. only *y-*) is added to the weak stem in the act., *-ī-* (before vowels *-īy-*) in the mid.

4. When the final sound of a stem is a consonant, the following phonetic rules apply: The endings *-s* and *-t* of the 2nd and 3rd sg. impf. act. disappear (§ 4 I), the final sound is treated according to § 4 III ff., cf. also the paradigm, § 63. For endings beginning with a consonant the rules in § 19 apply, before the endings beginning with *s* § 19 VI, 20 II apply. In the 3rd sg. impf. act. final dentals and *s* of the present stem after loss of the ending (s. above) become *t*, in the 2nd sg. impf. act. they become *t* or *ḥ*: *bhid-* "split" VII: *abhinat* (< *a-bhinad-t*) and *abhinat* or *abhinaḥ* (< *abhinad-s*); *śās-* II "order": *aśāt* and *aśāt* or *aśāḥ*.

§§ 63-64. Second (root-) class.

§ 63. The present stem is equal to the root; thus to this the personal endings are added, e.g., *vid-* "know": pres. st. strong: *ved-*, 1st sg. ind. act. *ved-mi*; weak *vid-*, 1st pl. ind. act. *vid-mas*.

Paradigm: *dviṣ-* "hate".

	Sg.	Du.	Pl.
		Indicative	
		Act.	
1st	*dveṣmi*	*dviṣvas*	*dviṣmas*
2nd	*dvekṣi* (§ 19 VI)	*dviṣṭhas*	*dviṣṭha*
3rd	*dveṣṭi* (§ 19 IV)	*dviṣṭas*	*dviṣanti*
		Mid.	
1st	*dviṣe*	*dviṣvahe*	*dviṣmahe*
2nd	*dvikṣe* (§ 19 VI)	*dviṣāthe*	*dviḍḍhve* (from -*ṣdh*-)
3rd	*dviṣṭe* (§ 19 IV)	*dviṣāte*	*dviṣate*
		Imperfect	
		Act.	
1st	*adveṣam*	*adviṣva*	*adviṣma*
2nd	*adveṭ* (§§ 4 I; V)	*adviṣṭam*	*adviṣṭa*
3rd	*adveṭ* (§§ 4 I; V)	*adviṣṭām*	*adviṣan*
		Mid.	
1st	*adviṣi*	*adviṣvahi*	*adviṣmahi*
2nd	*adviṣṭhās*	*adviṣāthām*	*adviḍḍhvam*
3rd	*adviṣṭa*	*adviṣātām*	*adviṣata*
		Optative	
		Act.	
1st	*dviṣyām*	*dviṣyāva*	*dviṣyāma*
2nd	*dviṣyās*	*dviṣyātam*	*dviṣyāta*
3rd	*dviṣyāt*	*dviṣyātām*	*dviṣyur*

	Sg.	Du.	Pl.
		Mid.	
1st	*dviṣīya*	*dviṣīvahi*	*dviṣīmahi*
2nd	*dviṣīthās*	*dviṣīyāthām*	*dviṣīdhvam*
3rd	*dviṣīta*	*dviṣīyātām*	*dviṣīran*
		Imperative	
		Act.	
1st	*dveṣāṇi*	*dveṣāva*	*dveṣāma*
2nd	*dviḍḍhi*	*dviṣṭam*	*dviṣṭa*
3rd	*dveṣṭu*	*dviṣṭām*	*dviṣantu*
		Mid.	
1st	*dveṣai*	*dveṣāvahai*	*dveṣāmahai*
2nd	*dvikṣva*	*dviṣāthām*	*dviḍḍhvam*
3rd	*dviṣṭām*	*dviṣātām*	*dviṣatām*

§ 64. I. From the root *vid-* "know" thus ind. act. *vedmi, vetsi, vetti, vidmas, vittha, vidanti*; in the 3rd pl. impf. act. always *avidur*; *dviṣ-* and the roots in *ā* can also have *-ur*: *adviṣur, ayur* (from *yā* "go" without the *ā* of the root).

II. Reduplicated roots of this class, e.g., *cakās-* "shine", have in the 3rd pl. ind. impf. imp. act. *-ati, -ur, -atu*: *cakāsati* "they shine"; in this way also *śās-* "order".

III. Paradigm of the root *i-* "go".

Act. ind. *emi, eṣi, eti, ivas, ithas, itas, imas, itha, yanti.*

Impf. (§ 57 V) *āyam, ais, ait, aiva, aitam, aitām, aima, aita, āyan.*

Imp. *ayāni, ihi, etu, ayāva, itam, itām, ayāma, ita, yantu.*

Opt. *iyām*, etc. The mid. with the preverb *adhi-* "study": *adhīye, adhīṣe, adhīte*, etc.

IV. To the root *duh-* "milk" belong: *dohmi, dhokṣi* (§ 4 note), *dogdhi, duhmas, dugdha, duhanti*; *lih-* "lick": *lehmi, lekṣi, leḍhi*

(§ 19 VII), *lihmas*, *līḍha* (§ 19 VII), *lihanti*; *ās-*, only mid. "sit": *āse*, *āsse*, *āste*, *āsmahe*, *ādhve*, *āsate*.

V. Paradigm of the root *as-* "be"; almost only in the active:
Ind. *asmi*, *asi*, *asti*, *svas*, *sthas*, *stas*, *smas*, *stha*, *santi*.
Impf. *āsam*, *āsīs*, *āsīt*, *āsva*, *āstam*, *āstām*, *āsma*, *āsta*, *āsan*.
Opt. *syām*, *syās*, *syāt*, *syāva*, *syātam*, *syātām*, *syāma*, *syāta*, *syur*.
Imp. *asāni*, *edhi*, *astu*, *asāva*, *stam*, *stām*, *asāma*, *sta*, *santu*.

VI. The roots *an-* "breathe", *rud-* "cry", *śvas-* "sigh", *svap-* "sleep", *jakṣ-* "eat" have *i* before the endings beginning with a consonant other than *y*, *ī* or *a* before the ending of the 2nd and 3rd sg. impf. act.; e.g., ind. *rodimi*, *rodiṣi*, *roditi*, *rudimas*, *ruditha*, *rudanti*; impf. *arodam*, *arodas*, or *arodīs*; opt. *rudyām*. These roots are *seṭ-* roots, s. § 71.

VII. The root *brū-* "speak" has *ī* in the strong forms before endings beginning with consonants: *bravīmi*, *bravīṣi*, *bravīti*, *brūmas*, *brūtha*, *bruvanti*; *abravam*, *abravīt*, *abruvan*; *brūyām*; *bravāṇi*, *brūhi*, *bravītu*; mid. *bruve*, *brūte*, etc.; cf. also § 18 I.

VIII. The roots ending in *u* have lengthened grade in the strong forms before endings beginning with consonants, thus *stu-* "praise": *staumi*, *stauṣi*, *stauti*; impf. *astavam* (*av* = *o*, § 18 II), *astaus*, *astaut*, 3rd pl. impf. *astuvan*; imp. *stavāni*, *stuhi*, *stautu*.

IX. The root *han-* "kill" forms the weak stem *han-* before *m*, *v*, *y*, *ha-* before endings beginning with other consonants, *ghn-* before vowels: *hanmi, haṃsi* (§ 19 VIII), *hanti, hanmas, hatha, ghnanti*; *ahanam, ahan, ahan, ahanma, ahata, aghnan*; *hanyām*; 2nd sg. imp. *jahi.*

X. To the root *śī-* "lie" belong: *śaye, śeṣe, śete, śemahe, śedhve, śerate*; *aśayi, aśethās,* 3rd pl. *aśerata.*

XI. The root *śās-* "order" forms the weak form *śiṣ-*: *śāsmi, śiṣmas,* 3rd pl. *śāsati*; opt. *śiṣyām,* 2nd sg. imp. *śādhi.* The root *mṛj-* "rub off, clean" forms *mārjmi, mārṣṭi.*

§§ 65-66. Third (reduplicating) class.

§ 65. The root is reduplicated; for the initial consonant, see § 57 VI; the vowel of the reduplication is the short form of the root vowel; *ṛ* and *ṝ* are, however, reduplicated by *i*: Thus: *bhī-* "be afraid": *bibhe-* strong pr. st., *bibhī-* weak pr. st.; *bhṛ-* "bear": *bibhar-, bibhṛ-*; *hu-* "sacrifice": *juho-, juhu-*.

To be noted are the endings *ati, ur, atu* in the 3rd pl. act. of the ind., impf., imp.; before *ur* a final vowel has the full grade.

Paradigm: *hu-* "pour into the fire, sacrifice".

Sg.	Du.	Pl.
	Indicative	
1st *juhomi*	*juhuvas*	*juhumas*
2nd *juhoṣi* (§ 21 II)	*juhuthas*	*juhutha*
3rd *juhoti*	*juhutas*	*juhvati* (§ 6)
	Mid.	
1st *juhve*	*juhuvahe*	*juhumahe*
2nd *juhuṣe*	*juhvāthe*	*juhudhve*
3rd *juhute*	*juhvāte*	*juhvate*
	Imperfect	
	Act.	
1st *ajuhavam*	*ajuhuva*	*ajuhuma*
2nd *ajuhos*	*ajuhutam*	*ajuhuta*
3rd *ajuhot*	*ajuhutām*	*ajuhavur*

	Sg	Du.	Pl.
		Mid.	
1st	*ajuhvi*	*ajuhuvahi*	*ajuhumahi*
2nd	*ajuhuthās*	*ajuhvāthām*	*ajuhudhvam*
3rd	*ajuhuta*	*ajuhvātām*	*ajuhvata*
		Imperative	
		Act.	
1st	*juhavāni*	*juhavāva*	*juhavāma*
2nd	*juhudhi* (exception!)	*juhutam*	*juhuta*
3rd	*juhotu*	*juhutām*	*juhvatu*
		Mid.	
1st	*juhavai*	*juhavāvahai*	*juhavāmahai*
2nd	*juhuṣva*	*juhvāthām*	*juhudhvam*
3rd	*juhutām*	*juhvātām*	*juhvatām*

Opt. act. *juhuyām,* etc.; mid. *juhvīya,* etc.

§ 66. The roots *dā-* "give" and *dhā-* "put" lose their root vowel in the weak forms: *dad-* and *dadh-*; with following *t* and *th* the final *dh* of *dadh-* becomes *tt* and *tth,* the initial sound is *dh* in these cases as well as in the forms with endings which begin with *s, h,* and *dh* (cf. § 4 note). Thus: *dā*: *dadāmi, dadāsi, dadmas, dattha, dadati,* etc.; 2nd sg. imp. *dehi* (in all forms like *dhā-*, only *d* instead of *dh*); *dhā-*: *dadhāmi, dadhmas, dhattha, dadhati*; mid. *dadhe, dhatse, dhatte, dadhmahe, dhaddhve, dadhate*; impf. *adadhām,* etc.; opt. *dadhyām,* mid. *dadhīya,* etc.; imp. *dadhāni, dhehi,* 2nd pl. *dhatta,* 2nd sg. mid. *dhatsva,* 2nd pl. *dhaddhvam.*

A few roots in *ā* have *i* in the reduplication syllable and in the weak forms change the *ā* into *ī,* which disappears before endings having initial vowels: *mā-* "measure" (only mid.): *mimī-*, *mim-*: ind. *mime*, *mimīṣe*, *mimīte*, 3rd pl. *mimate*; impf. *amimi*. *hā-* "leave" has as its weak stem *jahi-* or *jahī-* before endings beginning with consonants, *jah-* before endings beginning with vowels and in the opt.: ind. *jahāti*, *jahimas*, 3rd pl. *jahati*; impf. *ajahām*; opt. *jahyām*; 2nd imp. *jahāhi*, *jahīhi*, or *jahihi*.

§ 67. Fifth class.

In the weak forms *-nu-* is joined to the root, in the strong forms *-no-*: *su-* "press out": *sunu- suno-*. Before the endings beginning with *v* and *m* roots ending in a vowel can eliminate the *u* of the *nu*: *sunumas* or *sunmas*, but only *āpnumas*. These roots form the 2nd sg. imp. act. without *hi*: *sunu*; but *āpnuhi*. Roots with terminal consonants change *nu* into *nuv* before endings having initial vowels.

Paradigm: *su-* "press out".

	Sg.	Du.	Pl.
		Indicative	
		Act.	
1st	*sunomi*	*sunuvas* (*sunvas*)	*sunumas* (*sunmas*)
2nd	*sunoṣi*	*sunuthas*	*sunutha*
3rd	*sunoti*	*sunutas*	*sunvanti* (§ 6)
		Mid.	
1st	*sunve*	*sunuvahe* (*sunvahe*)	*sunumahe* (*sunmahe*)
2nd	*sunuṣe*	*sunvāthe*	*sunudhve*
3rd	*sunute*	*sunvāte*	*sunvate*

	Sg.	Du.	Pl.
		Imperfect	
		Act.	
1st	*asunavam* (§ 18 II)	*asunuva* (*asunva*)	*asunuma* (*asunma*)
2nd	*asunos*	*asunutam*	*asunuta*
3rd	*asunot*	*asunutām*	*asunvan*
		Mid.	
1st	*asunvi*	*asunuvahi* (*asunvahi*)	*asunumahi* (*asunmahi*)
2nd	*asunuthās*	*asunvāthām*	*asunudhvam*
3rd	*asunuta*	*asunvātām*	*asunvata*
		Imperative	
		Act.	
1st	*sunavāni*	*sunavāva*	*sunavāma*
2nd	*sunu*	*sunutam*	*sunuta*
3rd	*sunotu*	*sunutām*	*sunvantu*
		Mid.	
1st	*sunavai*	*sunavāvahai*	*sunavāmahai*
2nd	*sunuṣva*	*sunvāthām*	*sunudhvam*
3rd	*sunutām*	*sunvātām*	*sunvatām*

Opt. act. *sunuyām*, etc.; mid. *sunvīya*, etc.

To *āp-* "obtain" belong: *āpnomi*, 1st pl. *āpnumas*, 3rd pl. *āpnuvanti*. The Indians take the root *śru-* "hear" as the basis of the pr. st. *śṛṇu-*, strong *śṛṇo-*: *śṛṇomi*, *śṛṇoṣi*, *śṛṇumas* (*śṛṇmas*), *śṛṇvanti*.

§ 68. Seventh class. In the strong forms before the final consonant of the root *na-* (or *-ṇa-* § 20 I) is inserted, in the weak forms the nasal homorganic with this final consonant: *rudh-* "obstruct": *ruṇadh-, rundh-, yuj-* "join": *yunaj-, yuñj-*; before sibilants and *h* the inserted nasal is *ṃ*: *piṣ-* "crush": *pinas-, piṃṣ-*; in *hiṃs-* "hurt" the *ṃ* belongs to the root: strong *hinas-*, weak *hiṃs-*.

Paradigm: *bhid-* "split".

	Sg.	Du.	Pl.
		Indicative	
		Act.	
1st	*bhinadmi*	*bhindvas*	*bhindmas*
2nd	*bhinatsi* (§ 19 II)	*bhintthas*	*bhinttha*
3rd	*bhinatti* (§ 19 II)	*bhinttas*	*bhindanti*
		Mid.	
1st	*bhinde*	*bhindvahe*	*bhindmahe*
2nd	*bhintse*	*bhindāthe*	*bhinddhve*
3rd	*bhintte*	*bhindāte*	*bhindate*
		Imperfect	
		Act.	
1st	*abhinadam*	*abhindva*	*abhindma*
2nd	*abhinat* (*abhinas*)	*abhinttam*	*abhintta*
3rd	*abhinat*	*abhinttām*	*abhindan*
		Mid.	
1st	*abhindi*	*abhindvahi*	*abhindmahi*
2nd	*abhintthās*	*abhindāthām*	*abhinddhvam*
3rd	*abhintta*	*abhindātām*	*abhindata*
		Imperative	
		Act.	
1st	*bhinadāni*	*bhinadāva*	*bhinadāma*
2nd	*bhinddhi*	*bhinttam*	*bhintta*
3rd	*bhinattu*	*bhinttām*	*bhindantu*

	Sg.	Du.	Pl.
		Mid.	
1st	*bhinadai*	*bhinadāvahai*	*bhinadāmahai*
2nd	*bhintsva*	*bhindāthām*	*bhinddhvam*
3rd	*bhinttām*	*bhindātām*	*bhindatām*

Opt. act. *bhindyām*, etc.; mid. *bhindīya*, etc.
Thus: *yuj-*: *yunakti*, *yuṅkte*; *piṣ-*: *pinaṣṭi*, *piṃṣmas*.

§ 69. Eighth class. *u* is added to some roots in *n* in the weak stem, *o* in the strong stem: *tan-* "stretch": *tanu- tano-*. The inflection is like § 67 (*sunoti*). The root *kṛ-* "make" is irregular: weak st. *kuru-* (*kur-* before the endings beginning with *m*, *v*, *y*), strong st. *karo-*.

Paradigm *kṛ-* "make".

Ind. act. *karomi*, *karoṣi*, *karoti*, *kurvas*, *kuruthas*, *kurutas*, *kurmas*, *kurutha*, *kurvanti*; mid. *kurve*, *kuruṣe*, *kurute*, *kurvahe*, *kurvāthe*, *kurvāte*, *kurmahe*, *kurudhve*, *kurvate*.

Impf. act. *akaravam*, *akaros*, *akarot*, *akurva*, *akurutam*, *akurutām*, *akurma*, *akuruta*, *akurvan*; mid. *akurvi*, *akuruthās*, *akuruta*, *akurvahi*, *akurvāthām*, *akurvātām*, *akurmahi*, *akurudhvam*, *akurvata*.

Imp. act. *karavāṇi*, *kuru*, *karotu*, *karavāva*, *kurutam*, *kurutām*, *karavāma*, *kuruta*, *kurvantu*; mid. *karavai*, *kuruṣva*, *kurutām*, *karavāvahai*, *kurvāthām*, *kurvātām*, *karavāmahai*, *kurudhvam*, *kurvatām*.

Opt. act. *kuryām*, etc.; mid. *kurvīya*, etc.

§ 70. Ninth class. In the strong stem *-nā-* is added to the root (with *ṇ* instead of *n* according to § 20 I), in the weak stem *-nī-* (*n* before an ending beginning with a vowel). Paradigm *krī-* "buy": ind. act. *krīṇāmi*, etc., *krīṇīmas*, *krīṇītha*, *krīṇanti*; mid. *krīṇe*, *krīṇīṣe*, etc.; impf. act. *akrīṇām*, etc., *akrīṇīma*; imp. act. *krīṇāni*, *krīṇīhi*, *krīṇātu*, etc.; *jñā-* "know": ind. *jānāmi*, imp. *jānīhi*.

From roots which end in a consonant the 2nd sg. imp. act. in *āna* is formed: *grah-* "take": *gṛhāṇa* (ind. *gṛhṇāti*); thus the suffix disappears.

Paradigm: *aś-* "eat".

	Sg.	Du.	Pl.
		Indicative	
		Act.	
1st	*aśnāmi*	*aśnīvas*	*aśnīmas*
2nd	*aśnāsi*	*aśnīthas*	*aśnītha*
3rd	*aśnāti*	*aśnītas*	*aśnanti*
		Mid.	
1st	*aśne*	*aśnīvahe*	*aśnīmahe*
2nd	*aśnīṣe*	*aśnāthe*	*aśnīdhve*
3rd	*aśnīte*	*aśnāte*	*aśnate*
		Imperfect	
		Act.	
1st	*āśnām*	*āśnīva*	*āśnīma*
2nd	*āśnās*	*āśnītam*	*āśnīta*
3rd	*āśnāt*	*āśnītām*	*āśnan*
		Mid.	
1st	*āśni*	*āśnīvahi*	*āśnīmahi*
2nd	*āśnīthās*	*āśnāthām*	*āśnīdhvam*
3rd	*āśnīta*	*āśnātām*	*āśnata*
		Imperative	
		Act.	
1st	*aśnāni*	*aśnāva*	*aśnāma*

	Sg.	Du.	Pl.
2nd	*aśāna*	*aśnītam*	*aśnīta*
3rd	*aśnātu*	*aśnītām*	*aśnantu*
		Mid.	
1st	*aśnai*	*aśnāvahai*	*aśnāmahai*
2nd	*aśnīṣva*	*aśnāthām*	*aśnīdhvam*
3rd	*aśnītām*	*aśnātām*	*aśnatām*

Opt. act.: *aśnīyām*, etc.; mid. *aśnīya*, etc.

The root *jñā-* "recognize" forms the present *jānāti* (*jānīmas*, 3rd sg. ind. mid. *jānīte*). Roots in *ū* have the short vowel in the present: *pū-* "purify": *punāti* (*punīmas*, etc.). The root *bandh-* "bind" forms *badhnāti* (so also other stems with a nasal in the penult).

GENERAL TENSES

§ 71. Preliminary remarks. Indic grammar distinguishes between aniṭ [1])-roots, i.e., roots with which in the general tenses (i.e., the tenses outside of the present) and in the formation of verbal nouns the endings beginning with consonants except *y* are added directly to the root, and seṭ [1])-roots, which are formed with the "connecting vowel" *i* between the final sound of the root and the ending. The verb *grah-* "take" often has *ī* as the "connecting vowel".

A number of roots (in which *y*, *v*, or *r* precedes the vowel) are in imitation of the native grammarians not given in the weak grade as is usual (e.g., *dviṣ-* "hate", *bhid-* "split"), but in the full grade: *svap-* "sleep", *vyadh-* "bore through", *vac-*

[1]) *an-i-ṭ* means "without *i*", *seṭ* < *sa-i-ṭ* means "with *i*".

"speak"; the weak grade of these roots: *sup-*, *vidh-*, *uc-*, was called saṃprasāraṇa.

There are roots which form only certain tenses: from *as-* "be" only pres. and perf. are found, in the remaining tenses *bhū-* "become, etc." appears; *gā-* "go" forms the aorist of *i-* "go", for *dṛś-* "see" *paś-* IV is used as the present stem, etc.

FUTURE

§ 72. THE SIMPLE FUTURE. To the strong root *sya* is joined (according to § 20 II *ṣya*), to seṭ-roots *iṣya*. Almost only forms of the indicative are encountered. The inflection is the same as in the present. Paradigm: *dā-* "give": act. *dāsyāmi*, *dāsyasi*, *dāsyati*, *dāsyāmas*, *dāsyatha*, *dāsyanti*; mid. *dāsye*, *dāsyase*, *dāsyate*, *dāsyāmahe*, *dāsyadhve*, *dāsyante*. Paradigm: *kṛ-* "make": act. *kariṣyāmi*, *kariṣyasi*, etc.; mid. *kariṣye*, *kariṣyase*, etc. Further examples: *nī-* "lead": *neṣyati*, *bhū-* "become": *bhaviṣyati*, *śak-* "be able": *śakṣyati*, *labh-* "take": *lapsyate*, *tyaj-* "leave": *tyakṣyati*, *vas-* "dwell": *vatsyati*, *bhid-* "split": *bhetsyati*, *budh-* "awaken, recognize": *bhotsyate* (§ 4 note), *viś-* "enter": *vekṣyati* (§ 19 VI), *dṛś-* "see": *drakṣyati* (sic!), *gai-* "sing": *gāsyati*, *grah-* "take": *grahīṣyati*, *kṣam-* "forgive": *kṣaṃsyati* (§ 12 III). The verbs of the 10th class and the causatives (§§ 97; 98) keep the *ay* and add *iṣya* to it: *pātayati* "fell": *pātayiṣyati*.

Note. The conditional, which is formed from the future stem by prefixing the augment and with the endings of the imperfect, occurs only rarely: *dā-*: *adāsyat*.

§ 73. THE PERIPHRASTIC FUTURE consists of the nom. sg. of a *tṛ*-stem (noun of agent, § 29), to which in the 1st and 2nd person the forms of the ind. act. and mid. of *as-* "be" are added (there are, however, exceptions).

Paradigm: *dā-* "give".

	Sg.	Du.	Pl.
		Act. (du. and pl. rare)	
1st	*dātāsmi* (from *dātā* + *asmi*)	*dātāsvas*	*dātāsmas*
2nd	*dātāsi*	*dātāsthas*	*dātāstha*
3rd	*dātā*	*dātārau*	*dātāras*
		Mid. (rare)	
1st	*dātāhe*	*dātāsvahe*	*dātāsmahe*
2nd	*dātāse*	*dātāsāthe*	*dātādhve*
3rd	*dātā*	*dātārau*	*dātāras*

Thus: *dṛś-* "see": *draṣṭāsmi*, *grah-* "take": *grahītāsmi*, *jīv-* "live": *jīvitāsmi*, *bhū-* "become": *bhavitāsmi*. — Cf. also § 115.

Note. The masculine forms of the 3rd pers. are usually used for all genders.

AORIST

§ 74. There are in Sanskrit seven forms of the aorist, which are all formed by augmentation of the root and addition of the personal endings of the imperfect. The seven forms fall into simple and *s*-aorists. In post-Vedic texts the aorist, apart from some often used forms like *abhūt* "he was", etc., is used only little in the simple types of style; in the older language it is very frequent. In post-Vedic times one finds almost only indicative forms except the "injunctive" (§ 82).

§§ 75-77. Simple Aorists.

§ 75. The root aorist. This aorist is formed only from

some roots in *-ā* and diphthongs and from *bhū-*. The 3rd pl. loses the final vowel before the ending *ur*; *bhū-* becomes *bhūv-* before endings beginning with vowels and has *an* in the 3rd pl. Paradigm: *dā-* "give": *adām, adās, adāt, adāva, adātam, adātām, adāma, adāta, adur*; *bhū-* "become, etc.": *abhūvam, abhūs, abhūt, abhūma, abhūta, abhūvan.*

Note. The middle of the roots in *-ā* is inflected according to § 78.

§ 76. The thematic aorist. After the augmented weak root (only roots which end in *ṛ* or *ṝ* have full grade) follows the "thematic vowel" *a*; the inflection is that of the impf. of the 1st class (§ 60). This aorist exists beside many presents of the 4th class and beside some of the 1st and 6th classes; the middle is very rare. Paradigm: *sic-* "sprinkle": *asicam, asicas, asicat, asicāma, asicata, asican*; *krudh-* "be angry": *akrudhat*; exceptions: *dṛś-* "see": *adarśat*; *gam-* "go": *agamat.*

§ 77. The reduplicated aorist. The consonants are doubled according to § 57 VI; the inflection is in the act. and mid. that of the impf. of the 1st present class. The 3rd pl. act. has the ending *ur*. The root is weak. Final *i* and *u* go to *iy* and *uv*.

Examples: *pat-* "fall": *apaptam*, etc.; *dru-* "run": *adudruvam*; *vac-* "speak": *avocam* (from *a-va-uc-a-m*); *naś-* "pass away" has *aneśam*. This aorist is used especially beside pres. in *aya* and caus. (§§ 97; 98); *aya* does not occur in the aorist stem; the redupl. vowel is *i* or *ī*, with roots with *u* usually *u* or *ū*; the vowel of the reduplication has as a rule another quantity than that of the root syllable (— ⏑): *dṛś-* "see": *darśayati*: aor. *adīdṛśat, jan-*, caus. *janayati* "beget": aor. *ajījanat*; *budh-*, caus. *bodhayati* "awaken, instruct": aor. *abūbudhat.* A long root vowel is often shortened: *dīp-* "kindle", *dīpayati*: aor. *adīdipat*. The *p* of the causative (§ 97) also stands in the aorist: *jñā-*, caus. *jñāpayati* "instruct": *ajijñapat*.

§§ 78-81. SIGMATIC AORISTS.

§ 78. THE ATHEMATIC *s*-AORIST. This aorist is formed by adding *s* to the augmented root (according to § 20 II *ṣ*); the root vowel in the active is usually in the lengthened grade, in the middle with roots ending in *i*, *ī*, *u ū* in the full grade, but remains otherwise unchanged; only roots in *ā* and diphthongs which form the aor. mid. according to this form change *ā* into *i*. The endings are those of the imperfect; that of the 3rd pl. is *ur* in the act., *ata* in the mid.; the 2nd and 3rd sg. act. have the endings *īs*, *īt*. The sign of the aorist *s* is lost before the endings beginning with *t* and *th* after cons. except nasals and *r*, and always before *dhvam*, which becomes *ḍhvam* after all vowels except *a* and *ā* and after *r*. There are also forms without *s* which stem from the root aorist: *a-kṛ-ta*, *a-di-ta* (root *dā-*), 3rd sg. mid. This is the usual aorist of the aniṭ-roots (§ 71).

Paradigm: *ji-* "conquer"; *tud-* "push".

	Act.		Mid.	
			Sg.	
1st	*ajaiṣam*	*atautsam*	*ajeṣi*	*atutsi*
2nd	*ajaiṣīs*	*atautsīs*	*ajeṣṭhās*	*atutthās*
3rd	*ajaiṣīt*	*atautsīt*	*ajeṣṭa*	*atutta*
			Du.	
1st	*ajaiṣva*	*atautsva*	*ajeṣvahi*	*atutsvahi*
2nd	*ajaiṣṭam*	*atauttam*	*ajeṣāthām*	*atutsāthām*
3rd	*ajaiṣṭām*	*atauttām*	*ajeṣātām*	*atutsātām*

	Act.		Mid.	
		Pl.		
1st	*ajaiṣma*	*atautsma*	*ajeṣmahi*	*atutsmahi*
2nd	*ajaiṣṭa*	*atautta*	*ajeḍhvam*	*atuddhvam*
3rd	*ajaiṣur*	*atautsur*	*ajeṣata*	*atutsata*

Other examples: *kṛ-* "do, make": act. *akārṣam*, mid. *akṛṣi*, (3rd sg. *akṛta*, s. above); *śru-* "hear": *aśrauṣam*; *dṛś-* "see": *adrākṣam*; *sṛj-* "let loose": *asrākṣam, asṛkṣi*; *dā-* "give": mid. *adiṣi*.

§ 79. THE ATHEM. *iṣ*-AORIST. *iṣ* is added to the augmented root whose vowel appears in the full grade and, in the active with final vowel, in the lengthened grade. Of the roots with *a* before a simple consonant some have lengthened grade in the active, others optionally lengthened grade, still others full grade. The endings are the same as with the *s*-aorist. It is the regular aorist of the seṭ-roots (§ 71). Paradigm: *lū-* "cut off": act. *alāviṣam, alāvīs, alāvīt, alāviṣma, alāviṣṭa, alāviṣur*; mid. *alaviṣi, alaviṣṭhās, alaviṣṭa, alaviṣmahi, alavidhvam, alaviṣata*. Some examples: *budh-* "awaken, etc.": *abodhiṣam, abodhiṣi*; *kram-* "step": *akramiṣam*; *grah-* "seize": *agrahīṣam*.

§ 80. THE *siṣ*-AORIST. *siṣ* is added to the augmented root in full grade. It is found only with some roots in *ā*, diphthongs, and *am*; only in the active; in the middle these roots have the *iṣ*-aorist. Examples: *yā-* "go": *ayāsiṣam, ayāsīt*; *nam-* "bend": *anaṃsiṣam*.

§ 81. THE *sa*-AORIST. This aorist occurs only with roots which end in *ś, ṣ, h* (which always produce *kṣ* with the sign of the aorist *s* according to § 19 VI; 4 V) with a vowel other than *a* or *ā*. The inflection is the same as with the imperfect of the 1st cl., only the 1st sg. mid. ends in *i*, the 2nd and 3rd du. in *āthām* and *ātām*.Paradigm: *diś-* "show, give": act. *adikṣam, adikṣas, adikṣat, adikṣāma, adikṣata, adikṣan*; mid. *adikṣi, adikṣathās, adikṣata, adikṣāmahi, adikṣadhvam, adikṣanta.*

§ 82. INJUNCTIVE. There are aorist forms without augment which express prohibitions with the prohibitive *mā* "not": *mā gās* "do not go," *mā bhaiṣīs, mā bhais* "do not fear", *mā kārṣīs, mā kṛthās* "do not make".

§ 83. PRECATIVE. The rare precative is formed by adding in the active to the weak form of the root the mood-sign *yās* with athematic inflection; the root shows the changes mentioned with the passive (§ 95), only final *ā* is usually changed to *e*: *dā-* "give": *deyāsam*. Other examples: *bandh-* "bind": *badhyāsam, bhū-* "become": *bhūyāsam, bhūyās, bhūyāt, bhūyāsma, bhūyāsta, bhūyāsur*. Example of a middle form: *bhaviṣīya, bhaviṣīṣṭhās*, etc. from *bhū-*.

PERFECT

Sanskrit distinguishes the reduplicated and the periphrastic perfect. The non-derived verbs (cf. §§ 97 ff.) follow as a rule the reduplicating formation.

§§ 84-93. THE REDUPLICATED PERFECT.

§ 84. PRELIMINARY REMARKS. The perfect stem is formed by reduplication, and in fact with the roots beginning with consonants according to § 57 VI. The vowel of the reduplication syllable is the short or weak root vowel. The *ṛ* and the *ṝ* are, however, represented by *a*; likewise final diphthongs. Thus: *dā-* "give": *dadā-, kṛ-* "do, make": *cakṛ, puṣ-* "nourish":

pupuṣ-, *tap-* "heat": *tatap-*. With roots beginning with vowels initial *a* is lengthened to *ā* before simple consonants, e.g., *ad-* "eat": *ād-*; initial *a* before two consonants and initial *ṛ* prefix the syllable *ān* to themselves: *añj-* "besmear": *ānañj-*; *ṛdh-* "develop": *ānṛdh-* (there are only few cases); initial *ā* remains *ā*: *āp-* "obtain": *āp-*. Initial *i* and *u* become *ī* and *ū* in the weak perfect stem; in the strong stem *iy* and *uv* appear before the strong root vowel *e* or *o*: e.g., *iṣ-* "wish": weak pf. st. *īṣ-*, strong pf. st. *iyeṣ-*; *uṣ-* "burn": *ūṣ-* and *uvoṣ-*.

THE PERSONAL ENDINGS of the perfect are in the active: *-a*, *-tha*, *-a*; *-va*, *-athur*, *-atur*; *-ma*, *-a*, *-ur*; in the middle: *-e*, *-se*, *-e*; *-vahe*, *-āthe*, *-āte*; *-mahe*, *-dhve*, *-re*. The 3rd pl. mid. always has the vowel *i* before itself, the remaining endings beginning with cons. have it for most roots.

The three persons of the sg. act. are in general strong, all the rest are weak.

§ 85 PARADIGM OF THE ROOTS WITH *i*, *u*, OR *ṛ* before simple consonants; in the strong forms full grade of the vowel appears: *puṣ-* "nourish", *dṛś-* "see", *bhid-* "split".

	Act.		Mid.	
		Sg.		
1st	*puposa*	*dadarśa*	*bibhide*	*dadṛśe*
2nd	*pupoṣitha*	*dadarśitha*	*bibhidiṣe*	*dadṛśiṣe*
3rd	*pupoṣa*	*dadarśa*	*bibhide*	*dadṛśe*
		Du.		
1st	*pupuṣiva*	*dadṛśiva*	*bibhidivahe*	*dadṛśivahe*
2nd	*pupuṣathur*	*dadṛśathur*	*bibhidāthe*	*dadṛśāthe*
3rd	*pupuṣatur*	*dadṛśatur*	*bibhidāte*	*dadṛśāte*

	Act.		Mid.	
		Pl.		
1st	*pupuṣima*	*dadṛśima*	*bibhidimahe*	*dadṛśimahe*
2nd	*pupuṣa*	*dadṛśa*	*bibhididhve*	*dadṛśidhve*
3rd	*pupuṣur*	*dadṛśur*	*bibhidire*	*dadṛśire*

§ 86. Roots with *a* before simple consonants have lengthened grade optionally in the 1st sg. act., always in the 3rd sg., full grade in the 2nd sg.: *tap-* "heat, etc." 1st sg. *tatapa* or *tatāpa*, 3rd sg. *tatāpa*; *kram-* "step": *cakrama* or *cakrāma*, *cakramitha*, *cakrāma*; cf. § 90.

§ 87. Roots with *a* between consonants (thus type *pac-* "cook"), of which the initial one is reduplicated with itself (thus not *has-* "laugh", for *h* has the representative *j* in the reduplication: *jahas-*) form the weak stem by the unreduplicated root with *e* instead of *a*. If in the 2nd sg. act. the ending is added by means of *i*, then the weak stem appears with these verbs. Roots which begin with two consonants remain unchanged in the weak stem. Paradigm: *pac-* "cook".

	Sg.	Du.	Pl.
		Act.	
1st	*papāca* or *papaca*	*peciva*	*pecima*
2nd	*pecitha* or *papaktha*	*pecathur*	*peca*
3rd	*papāca*	*pecatur*	*pecur*
		Mid.	
1st	*pece*	*pecivahe*	*pecimahe*
2nd	*peciṣe*	*pecāthe*	*pecidhve*
3rd	*pece*	*pecāte*	*pecire*

From the root *kram-* "step" are derived however the act.

cakrama, etc.; mid. *cakrame*; from *gam-* "go": act. *jagama*, etc., *jagmima, jagma, jagmur*; mid. *jagme*, etc.; *jan-* "be born": *jajñe*. Exceptions: *bhaj-* "distribute, allot" has *bheje*; from *rāj-* "shine" is found *rejur*, etc.

§ 88. SOME ROOTS WITH NON-INITIAL *y* OR *v* BEFORE VOWEL run as follows: *svap-* "sleep": act. *suṣvāpa*, etc., mid. *suṣupe* (*ṣ*, § 20 II); *vyadh-* "pierce": *vivyādha*, 3rd pl. *vividhur*; *grah-* "seize" forms *jagrāha, jagṛhe*.

§ 89. I. SOME ROOTS BEGINNING WITH *va* have *uva* in the strong stem and *ū* instead of *va* in the weak stem. Paradigm: *vac-* "speak":

	Sg.	Du.	Pl.
		Act.	
1st	*uvāca* or *uvaca*	*ūciva*	*ūcima*
2nd	*uvacitha* or *uvaktha*	*ūcathur*	*ūca*
3rd	*uvāca*	*ūcatur*	*ūcur*
		Mid.	
1st	*ūce*	*ūcivahe*	*ūcimahe*
2nd	*ūciṣe*	*ūcāthe*	*ūcidhve*
3rd	*ūce*	*ūcāte*	*ūcire*

II. In the same way is conjugated *yaj-* "sacrifice": *iyāja*, etc.; *īje*, etc.

III. The root *iṣ-* "wish" has *iyeṣa, īṣima*; *īṣe* (§ 84).

§ 90. OF ROOTS IN *i, ī, u, ū, ṛ, ṝ* the strong stem has optionally full or lengthened grade in the 1st sg. act., full grade in the 2nd sg., lengthened grade in the 3rd sg.: *stu-* "praise": *tuṣṭāva* or *tuṣṭava, tuṣṭotha, tuṣṭāva, tuṣṭuma, tuṣṭuva, tuṣṭuvur* (§ 18 I); *nī-* "lead": *ināya, ninyur* (§ 6); *ji-* "conquer" forms *jigāya*.

In the weak stem the roots in *ṛ* after several consonants and most in *ṝ* have full grade: *smṛ-* "remember": 3rd pl. act. *sasmarur*.

The root *i-* "go" forms *iyāya, īyur*.

§ 91. Roots in *ā* and diphthongs have the ending *au* in the 1st and 3rd sg. act.; in the weak forms (and optionally in the 2nd sg. act.) they have the vowel *i* before an ending beginning with a cons., no root vowel before an ending beginning with a vowel. Paradigm: *dā-* "give".

	Sg.	Du.	Pl.
		Act.	
1st	*dadau*	*dadiva*	*dadima*
2nd	*dadātha* or *daditha*	*dadathur*	*dada*
3rd	*dadau*	*dadatur*	*dadur*
		Mid.	
1st	*dade*	*dadivahe*	*dadimahe*
2nd	*dadiṣe*	*dadāthe*	*dadidhve*
3rd	*dade*	*dadāte*	*dadire*

§ 92. Roots beginning and ending with a consonant and simultaneously prosodically long have no gradation: *nind-* "blame" has in all forms *ninind-*, *jīv-* "live" *jijīv-* (§ 3 end).

§ 93. The root *vid-* has no reduplication in the meaning "know": *veda* "I know", *vettha, veda, vidma, vida, vidur.*

The perfect of the root *bhū-* "become, etc." is irregular: *babhūva, babhūvitha, babhūva, babhūvima, babhūva, babhūvur.* The forms of the root *ah-* "say" are incomplete only in the act.: sg. 2nd *āttha*, 3rd *āha*, du. *āhathur, āhatur*, pl. *āhur*.

§ 94. The periphrastic perfect. This construction is

used principally with the derived verbs, especially with the causative; also roots which begin with a prosodically long vowel except *a* and *ā* and *ās-* "sit" form this perfect. It is formed by adding the invariable *ām* to the present stem; this form is combined with the perfect forms of *kṛ-* "make" (act. and mid.), *as-* "be" or *bhū-* "become, etc." (only act.). Examples: *tuṣ-*: caus. (§ 97) *toṣayati* "satisfy": *toṣayāmāsa*; *īkṣ-* "see": *īkṣāṃcakre*; *ās-* "sit": *āsāṃcakre*; *mā-* "measure" (III *mimīte*), *māpayati* "cause to be measured, cause to be built": *māpayāṃcakre*.

THE PASSIVE

§ 95. The present.

I The syllable *ya* is added to the root with the personal endings of the middle; the inflection is that of the 1st pres. class, e.g., *dviṣ-* "hate": *dviṣ-ya-te*; *yuj-* "yoke, join": *yujyate*.

The passive stem has the weak grade of the root: *dviṣyate*; *bandh-* "bind": *badhyate*; *vac-* "speak": *ucyate*, *vas-* "dwell": *uṣyate*, *grah-* "seize": *gṛhyate*; *nind-* "blame": *nindyate*. Final vowels are changed and in fact as follows: final *ā* and diphthongs usually go to *ī*: *dā-* "give": *dīyate*; *gai-* "sing": *gīyate*; but *jñā-* "know": *jñāyate*; *dhyai-* "consider": *dhyāyate*; final *i* and *u* become *ī* and *ū*: *ci-* "gather": *cīyate*, *śru-* "hear": *śrūyate*; *ṛ* becomes *ri* after simple cons., *ar* after two cons.: *kṛ-* "do": *kriyate*, *smṛ-* "remember": *smaryate*; *ṝ* becomes *īr*, after labials *ūr*: *śṝ-* "break": *śīryate*; *pṝ-* "fill": *pūryate*. Passive of *hve-* "call": *hūyate*. The present of the root *jan-* "be born", *jāyate* is intrans. mid. of the 4th pr. cl. Several passives are originally intransitives; they frequently have intrans. meaning.

II. The passive belonging to the presents of the 10th class and caus. (§ 97) is formed without the syllable *ay*: *lakṣayati* "notice": *lakṣyate*; *vādayati* "cause to be spoken, cause to be sounded (from *vad-* "speak"): *vādyate*. It should be noted that the root vowel of the caus. remains.

§ 96. General Tenses. Here the middle also has the meaning of a passive. Only a 3rd sg. aor. pass. in *i* is found: *lū-* "cut off": *alāvi*, *pac-* "cook": *apāci*, *diś-* "show": *adeśi*, *dṛś-* "see": *adarśi*, *jan-* "be born": *ajani*, *dhā-* "put": *adhāyi* (likewise the other roots in *ā*).

THE DERIVED VERBAL STEMS

§ 97. Causatives. In general every verb can form a present with causative meaning beside its present class: *aya* is added to the root whose vowel, if it is final, shows as a rule lengthened grade (often also if it is *a* before a cons.), but if it occurs medially before a cons., it has the full grade. The inflection is that of the 1st present class. Examples: *kṛ-* "make": *kārayati* "cause to be made", *nī-* "lead": *nāyayati* "cause to be led", *pat-* "fall": *pātayati* "cause to fall, fell", *tuṣ-* "be pleased": *toṣayati* "satisfy". There are, however, a number of roots with internal *a* before a cons. which do not lengthen the *a*: *jan-* "be born": *janayati* "beget", etc. Most roots ending in *ā* have *paya* as a causative sign: *dā-* "give": *dāpayati* "cause to be given"; some run like *jñā-* "know": *jñāpayati* or *jñapayati* "inform". Also *ṛ-* "go" forms *arpayati* "fasten, offer"; *ruh-* "grow, climb" has *ropayati* beside *rohayati*, *adhi-i-* "learn": *adhyāpayati* "instruct"; *kṣi-* "destroy" has *kṣayayati* and *kṣapayati*. The root *sidh-* "succeed" forms *sādhayati* "accomplish".

Irregular are e.g., *dūṣayati* "damage" and *pūrayati* "fill".

§ 98. Tenth present class. There are a number of verbs which form the present without causative meaning according to the *aya-* conjugation; many are denominatives. Examples: *amitrayati* "be hostile" (from *amitra-* "hostile"), *varṇayati* "describe" (from *varṇa-* "color"), *corayati* "steal".

The future of the *aya*-verbs has *ay* + *iṣya*: from *kṛ-*: *kārayiṣyati*. Concerning aor., pert., and pass. one should refer to §§ 77; 94; 95 II.

§ 99. Desideratives. *sa*, sometimes *iṣa-*, is added to the reduplicated root. The reduplication syllable has *i* as a vowel, but *u* if the root syllable contains *u* or *ū* or gets *ū* according to the following rule. Examples: *pā-* "drink": *pipāsati* "wish to drink", *jīv-* "live": *jijīviṣati* "wish to live", *dṛś-* "see": *didṛkṣati* (§ 19 VI) "wish to see". Final *i* goes to *ī*, final *u* to *ū*, final *ṛ* and *ṝ* go to *īr*, after labials to *ūr*: *śru-* "hear": *śuśrūṣati*, *kṛ-* "make": *cikīrṣati*, pres. part. mid. *cikīrṣamāṇa-*, *mṛ-* "die": *mumūrṣati*. The root *grah-* "seize" forms *jighṛkṣati*, *cit-* "observe", *cikitsati* "heal", *han-* "kill" *jighāṃsati*. Some desideratives have obtained greater independence: *bhikṣ-* "beg" (wish to get)" from *bhaj-* "obtain", etc. Cf. also § 116 III.

§ 100. Intensives. The intensive stem has a reduplication strengthened by full grade, lengthening, or in another way, and the suffix *ya*. The inflection is that of the middle of the 1st class. The treatment of final root vowels is the same as with the passive. Examples: *dīp-* "shine": *dedīpyate*; *rū-* "cry": *rorūyate* "cry repeatedly or very much"; *mṛj-* "rub off": *marmṛjyate*.

There are also other intensive formations, e.g., *vid-* "know": *vevetti*; *kram-* "step": *caṅkramīti*.

VERBAL NOUNS

§ 101. PARTICIPLES OF THE TENSE STEMS.

I. IN THE PRES. AND FUT. OF THE ACT. the suffix is *at* in the weak participial stem, *ant* in the strong stem; in the future and thematic present stems only *a* stands instead of *a* of the suffix with the thematic vowel *a*. Inflection, s. § 36. Thus: in the pres. of the thematic conjugation *bhṛ-* I *bharati* "bear": strong *bharant-*, weak *bharat-*; *tuṣ-* IV *tuṣyati* "be pleased": strong *tuṣyant-*, weak *tuṣyat-*; in the pres. of the athematic conj. the suffix is added to the weak present stem: *dviṣ-* II *dveṣṭi* "hate": *dviṣant-*, *dviṣat-*; *bhid-* VII *bhinatti* "split": *bhindant-*, *bhindat-*; *aś-* IX *aśnāti* "eat"; *aśnant-*, *aśnat-*. Reduplicated stems have only the weak stem: *hu-* III *juhoti* "sacrifice": cf. § 37. Part. fut. act. *bhū-* "become, etc." *bhaviṣyati*: *bhaviṣya(n)t-*.

II. IN THE PRES. MID. of the thematic conjugation and in the pres. of the passive *māna* (according to § 20 I *māṇa*) is added to the pres. stem: *bhara-māṇa-*; pass. *tud-ya-māna*. In the athematic conj. *āna* (*āṇa*, § 20 I) is added to the weak pres. stem: *bhid-* VII: *bhindāna-*; *hu-* III: *juhvāna-*, *brū-* II: *bruvāṇa-*, *śī-* II "lie": *śayāna-*, *kṛ-* VIII: *kurvāṇa-*. Irregular is *ās-* II "sit": *āsīna-*. Part. fut. mid.: *dā-*: *dāsyamāna-*.

III. IN THE PERF. PART. OF THE ACT. *vas* (§ 42) is added to the weak perf. stem; it is added to monosyllabic perf. stems with the vowel *i* except in the weak prevocalic declension stem. Thus *kṛ-*: *cakṛvas-*, *jan-* "be born": *jajñivas-*, weak prevocalic stem *jajñuṣ-*, *pac-* "cook": *pecivas-*, *pecuṣ-*; but *vid-*: *vidvas-*.

IV. IN THE PERF. PART. OF THE MIDDLE *āna* (*āṇa*) is added to the weak stem: *kṛ-*: *cakrāṇa-*, *pac-*: *pecāna-*.

§ 102 VERBAL ADJECTIVES FROM THE ROOT OR THE DERIVED VERBAL STEM. There are verbal adjectives (also called participles) in *ta* and *na*; for intransitive verbs they have preterital meaning, whereas in the case of transitive verbs the meaning is usually pret. and passive, sometimes active also.

Examples: *ciraṃ supto 'smi* "I have slept long"; *rājā gṛhaṃ gataḥ* "the king has gone home"; *ghaṇṭā mayā dattā* "the bell has been given by me, I have given the bell".

The suffixes *-ta-* and *-na-* are added to the weak root (note §§ 19 III-V; VII): *bhṛ-* I *bharati*: *bhṛta-*, *yuj-* VII "yoke": *yukta-*, *svap-* "sleep": *supta-*, *vac-* "speak": *ukta-*, *yaj-* "honor the gods by a sacrifice": *iṣṭa-*. Seṭ-roots ending in a consonant have the vowel *i* before *ta*, not before *na*: *pat-* "fall": *patita-*, but *dah-* "burn": *dagdha-* (§ 19 III), *grah-* (§ 71): *gṛhīta-*, *guh-* "hide": *gūḍha-*, etc., *vah-* "lead": *ūḍha-*.

One should note: instead of final *ā* and *ai* of some roots we find *ī*: *pā-* "drink": *pīta-*, with other roots *i*: *sthā-* "stand": *sthita-*; *dhā-* "put" forms *hita-*; *jñā-* "know", *yā-* "go", *khyā-* "name", etc. retain the *ā*: *khyāta-*. The suffix *ta* is always added with the vowel *i* to the stems of the 10th cl. and the caus. after loss of *aya*: *tuṣ-*: caus. *toṣayati* "satisfy": *toṣita-*. Note *ā-jñā-* X "order": *ājñapta-*.

If a root ends in *a* and a nasal, then *a* appears: *gam-* "go": *gata-*, *man-* "think, consider": *mata-*; but they frequently have long vowel + *n*: *kram-* "step": *krānta-*; some have only *ā*: *khan-* "dig": *khāta-*; *jan-* "be born": *jāta-*. But *daṃś-* "bite": *daṣṭa-* (§ 19 V).

The root *dā-* "give" forms *datta-*; *prach-* "ask": *pṛṣṭa-*, *ghas-* "eat": *jagdha-*.

Some roots form the verbal adj. optionally with *ta* or *na*: *tvar-* "hasten": *tvarita-* and *tūrṇa-*.

The rarer *na* (*ṇa*) is added to the roots in *ṝ*: *tṝ-* "step over": *tīrṇa-*, *pṝ-* "fill": *pūrṇa-*; to most in *d*: *pad-* "get into": *panna-*; to some roots ending in a vowel: *hā-* "leave": *hīna-*, etc ; to some roots in *g* and *j* (*j* goes to *g* before *na*): *lag-* "hang": *lagna-*; *vij-* "be frightened": *vigna*, *bhañj-* "break": *bhagna-*, *majj-* "sink under": *magna-*.

§ 103. There is a VERBAL ADJECTIVE WITH ACTIVE PRETERITAL MEANING which is often used in the sense of a finite verb: it is formed by addition of *vat* (declension: § 38) to the just mentioned perf. pass. part.: *ukta-vat-* "having said", *uktavān* (nom. sg. m.): "(he) said". Periphrastic construction: *kṛtavāṃs tvaṃ bhaviṣyasi* "you will have made".

§ 104. GERUNDIVE (cf. § 116 VII). There are three formations:

a) *tavya* to the full grade of the root, with seṭ-roots together with *i*: *kṛ-*: *kartavya-*; *bhū-*: *bhavitavya-* ("what should be"); the *aya*-stems retain the *ay*: *budh-* caus.: *bodhayitavya-*.
b) *anīya* (*aṇīya* § 20 I), usually to the root in the full grade: *kṛ-*: *karaṇīya-*; the *aya*-stems lose the *ay*: *cint-* X "think": *cintanīya-*.
c) *ya*: *dā-*: *deya-*; *bhū-*: *bhavya-* or *bhāvya-* "what should happen"; *kṛ-* "do": *kārya-*; *vadh-* "kill": *vadhya-*, *labh-* "obtain": *labhya-*; *cint-* X: *cintya-*; *sthā-* caus. *sthāpayati*: *sthāpya-*. After some roots in *i u ṛ* also *tya*: *kṛtya-*.

§ 105. INFINITIVE. *tum* is added to the full grade of the

root, with seṭ-roots together with *i*: *kr̥-* "make": *kartum, yuj-* "yoke" VII: *yoktum, dr̥ś-* "see": *draṣṭum* (sic!); *jīv-* "live": *jīvitum, sah-* "bear": *soḍhum, grah-* "take": *grahītum*; *ji-* "conquer": *jetum*; *bhū-* "become": *bhavitum*; *gam-* "go": *gantum*; *tr̥̄-* "cross over": *taritum* or *tarītum*. The *aya*-verbs retain the *ay* and add *i*; *budh-* caus.: *bodhayitum*.

§ 106. Gerunds. Besides the rare formation with *am* (*kr̥-*: *kāram*) Old Indic has two gerunds which are used as indeclinable participles and designate an action which precedes the action expressed by the principal verb of the sentence; the grammatical or logical subject of the sentence is the agent of the gerund.

The gerund I in *tvā* is that of the uncompounded verbs. With regard to the root form and the *i* before *tvā* the same rules apply as with *ta*; roots in *r̥̄* are treated as with the passive. *kr̥-*: *kr̥tvā*; *vac-* "speak": *uktvā, dr̥ś-* "see": *dr̥ṣṭvā, svap-* "sleep": *suptvā, grah-*: *gr̥hītvā, han-* "kill": *hatvā, sthā-*: *sthitvā, kram-* "step": *krāntvā*. The *aya*-stems retain *ay*: *budh-*: *bodhayitvā* "having drawn one's attention".

The gerund II in *ya* is added to verbs which are compounded with preverbs (prepositions); in epic now and then also to simple verbs. The rules given above (§ 95) for the passive concerning the form of the root are applicable: *vi-muc-* "free": *vimucya*; *pra-vas-* "set out": *proṣya* (from *pra-uṣ-ya*). Final *ā* remains unchanged: *pra-dā-* "give": *pradāya*. Roots in a short vowel have *tya*: *abhi-dru-* "run towards": *abhi-drutya*. The roots in *am* and *an*, as they have *a* instead of *am* or *an* in the weak grade, can likewise add *tya*: *ā-gam-* "come": *āgatya* beside *āgamya*; some always have it: *ni-han-* "strike down": *nihatya*; *jan-* "be born" and *khan-* "dig" form *-jāya* and -*khāya* beside -*janya* and -*khanya*. The *aya*-verbs lose *ay*: *vi-bhāvayati* "disclose": *vibhāvya*; they retain it only if the preceding root syllable is prosodically short: *sam-gamayati* "bring together": *saṃgamayya*.

COMPOSITION

§ 107. VERBAL COMPOSITION.

I. By compounding with one or more preverbs the meaning of verbs often is modified:

ati "over, beyond, past": *carati* "go": *aticarati* "go past, pass over".

adhi "over, on": *adhikaroti* "put over something".

anu "along, after": *eti* (*i-* § 64 III) "go": *anveti* "go after, follow".

antar (rare) "in between, etc.": *antardadhāti* (*dhā-* § 66) "put in between".

apa "away, off": *apanayati* (*nī-* I) "lead away".

api "near to, at, on": *apidadhāti* (§ 66) "cover up, close".

abhi "to, unto, toward": *abhidravati* (*dru-* I) "run towards, draw near".

ava "down, from, away": *avatarati* (*tṝ-*) "climb down".

ā "hither, unto": *gacchati* (§ 61 I) "go": *āgacchati* "come"; *dadāti* (§ 66) "give": *ādatte* "take"; *nī-*, *nayati* "lead": *ānayati* "bring near, take along".

ud "up, up forth, forth; out": *udeti* "go up, go out, arise".

upa "to, unto": *upaiti* (*upa* + *eti*, § 5 II) "arrive at".

ni "down, into": *nipatati* "fall down".

nis "out, away from": *niṣkramati* "go out".

parā "away, off, aside, etc.": *parāvartate* "turn back, return".

pari "around": *kṣipati* VI "throw": *parikṣipati* "surround, enclose"; also intensive meaning: *parijayati* (*ji-* I) "conquer (completely)".

pra "before, forward": *pravahati* "travel farther", also initial stage: *prahasati* "burst out laughing".

prati "against, back": *bhāṣate* "speak": *pratibhāṣate* "answer".

vi "asunder, away": *yunakti* "join": *viyunakti* "separate".

sam "together"; *saṃgacchati* "come together, unite with"; also intensive meaning: *saṃyacchati* (*yam-*, § 61 I) "bridle".

Some adverbs can be compounded with a limited number of verbs: *alaṃkaroti* "decorate", etc.

II. Nouns can be compounded with the auxiliary verbs *kṛ-* "make", *bhū-* "become", *as-* "be"; final *a* and *an* of the nominal stems go to *ī*, *i* goes to *ī*, *u* to *ū*, etc.; the meaning is "turn into something, become, be": *bahulībhavati* "multiply", *ekībhavati* "unite".

§§ 108-113. Nominal Composition.

§ 108. Preliminary remarks. Nominal compounds are very frequent in Sanskrit. With exception of the dvandvas (s. § 109) they always consist of only two members; but they can themselves again become members of a new compound. With exception of the final member all members in general assume the stem form; nominal stems with gradation have weak grade in their preconsonantal form. Pronouns have the forms of their stems mentioned in §§ 47 ff. Instead of *mahat-* "great" we find *mahā* in the first member of a karmadhāraya or bahuvrīhi (§§ 111; 112); final members sometimes become *a*-stems: *mahārāja-* "a great king" instead of *mahat-* + *rājan-* "king". The rules of sentence sandhi (above §§ 5 ff.) with some easily understandable exceptions apply to compounds.

§ 109. Dvandva (copulative compounds). In these compounds two or more members are coordinated; they can usually be decomposed into their constituent elements and then connected by "and". The compound is either:

a) dual or plural, according as two or more persons or things are designated: *hastyaśvau* "an elephant (*hastin-*) and a horse (*aśva-*)"; *hastyaśvāḥ* "elephants and horses"; *suta-bhārye* "son (*suta-*) and wife (*bhāryā-*)"; such a dvandva thus has the gender of the last member; *vṛka-siṃha-vyāghrāḥ*, "wolves, lions, and tigers", *prāṇāpānodāneṣu* "with exhaling, inhaling, breathing again", or:

b) a collective neuter in the singular, often two abstracts like *sukhaduḥkham* "joy and pain"; *aharniśam* "day (*ahan-*) and night (*niśā-*)".

Adjectival dvandva compounds also occur: *vṛttapīna-* "round and fat".

§ 110. Tatpuruṣa (determinative compounds). A tatpuruṣa compound is subst. or adj., according as the final member is subst. or adj. The last member is defined more exactly by the first member. The first member can represent every oblique case: *pṛthivī-pāla-* "lord of the earth" (gen. sg.), *aśva-kovida-* "skilled in horses" (gen. pl.), *svarga-gati-* "ascension to heaven" (acc.), *deva-gupta-* "protected by the god or by the gods" (instr.), *svarga-patita-* "fallen from heaven" (abl.). It should be noted that a root can occur in the final member with the meaning of a participle: *brahma-vid-* "knowing divine knowledge"; roots in a short vowel get final *t*: *sarva-ji-t-* "conquering the universe"; roots in *ā* frequently shorten this: *veda-jña-* "knowing the Veda" (*jñā-*); roots in a nasal often go over to the *a*-class: *grāma-ja-* "born (*jan-*) in a village". There are also tatp. comp. with a case form in the first member: *divas-pati-* (d. § 31) "lord of heaven", *divi-kṣit-* "living in heaven".

§ 111. KARMADHĀRAYA (APPOSITIONALLY DEFINED COMPOUNDS). Here the final member is defined more exactly by the first member as an attribute, apposition, or comparison, or the first member designates the species, the second the genus. There are four types: adj. (adv.) + subst. *nīlotpala-* "blue (*nīla-*) lotus (*u.*)"; *su-yajña-* "beautiful sacrifice"; subst. + adj. *megha-śyāma-* "black like a cloud"; subst. + subst. *rājarṣi-* (*rāja-* + *ṛṣi-*) "a seer who is a king"; *kanyā-ratna-* "a girl like a jewel"; *cūta-vṛkṣa-* "mango tree". Native grammar considers under the determ. comp. also: adj. + adj. *dṛṣṭa-naṣṭa-* "scarcely seen, already vanished", *pīta-rakta-* "yellowish red". — If the first member is a numeral, then the comp. is called dvigu: *tri-loka-* "three worlds".

§ 112. BAHUVRĪHI (POSSESSIVE COMPOUNDS). These comp. are always adj., but their final member is always a subst. The subst. to which they are joined determines their gender. The first member is:

a) an adj. (part., numeral): *bahu-vrīhi-* "he whose rice is much" (*vrīhir bahur yasya, saḥ*); *gatāyus-* "he from whom life (*āyus-*) has gone; dead";
b) a subst.: *tapo-dhana-* "he whose wealth is asceticism";
c) an indeclinable: *dur-bala-* "he whose strength is bad; weak"; *a-bala-* "without strength" (*balaṃ yasya nasti, saḥ*); *sa-bhārya-* (thus *-ă-*!) "accompanied by the wife (*bhāryā*)".

Sometimes *ka* is added: *sāgnika-* (*sa-agni-ka-*) "accompanied by Agni". — Expressions which mean "hand" (also other parts of the body) stand in last place: *daṇḍa-pāṇi-* "having a stick in the hand" (*daṇḍaḥ pāṇau yasya, saḥ* or *daṇḍena pāṇir yasya, saḥ*); the comp. then designates that one who holds or has attached at this part of the body the entity mentioned in the first member. — Bah. comp. with an infinitive stem as the first member, *manas-* or *kāma-* as the final member are frequent: *vaktumanas-* "intending to say": *ahaṃ vaktumanās* "I am intending to say"; *tyaktukāma-* "wishing to leave".

§ 113. AVYAYĪBHĀVA (ADVERBIAL COMPOUNDS). A. are indeclinable, adverbially used compounds whose first member is an indeclinable and whose second member is a noun which takes the ending of the acc. sg. neutr. (often *-am*): *sa-kopam* (*kopa-* m. "anger") "angrily", *praty-aham* (*ahan-* § 45 I) "daily", *yathecchham* (*yathā* "as" + *icchā* "wish") "according to desire".

SOME REMARKS ON SYNTAX

A few important characteristics only are mentioned.

§ 114. CASE AND NUMBER.

I. THE COPULA *as-* "be" is usually omitted if the predicate is a noun: *yathā vṛkṣas tathā phalam* "as the tree (is), so (is) the fruit".

II. THE ACCUSATIVE designates not only the object of a transitive verb but also the destination of a motion: *Takṣaśilāṃ pratasthe* "he departed for T.", and the extent of space and time: *pratīkṣasva kaṃcit kālam,* "wait some time". The acc. of an abstract in *tā* or *tva* can occur with verbs of motion in the sense of "become something": *vṛddhatāṃ gacchati* "he is becoming old". After verbs of speaking, asking, teaching, etc. a double acc. is possible: *devān papracchur enaṃ Kurupu-trāḥ* "the sons of Kuru made inquiries of him about the gods". The Latin acc. with infinitive does not exist in Sanskrit; but we frequently find the acc. with a participle after verbs of sensual and mental perception: *tam āgacchantam apaśyam* "I saw him coming", or a double acc.: *taṃ balinam apaśyam* "I saw that he was strong". The sg. cognate acc. is frequently found: *tapas tapate* "he practices asceticism". The acc. is dependent on the preposition in *Damayantīm anu-vrataḥ* "devoted to D.".

III. THE INSTRUMENTAL designates means, instrument: *vastreṇa channaḥ* "covered with a dress"; reason or cause: *lajjayā na kiṃcid abhāṣata* "due to modesty she said nothing"; the agent with the passive: *tena kathānakaṃ prārabdham* "by him a story was begun"; the accompanying or associated person or thing: *ahaṃ tvayā gamiṣyāmi vanam* "I shall go with you to the forest" (very often, especially in post-Vedic prose with *saha, sārdham, sahita-*, etc. "with"); also with verbs of separation: *śarīreṇa viyujyate* "he frees himself from the body"; for the designation of equality and similarity: *tena tulyaḥ* "equal to him"; of the value or price: *tad bahumūlyena krītam* "this has been bought for a large sum of money"; of characteristic (distinguishing mark, attributes, manner and way, etc.): *keśaiḥ sitaiḥ* "with white hair"; of criterion: *audāryeṇa* "on the basis of (his) magnanimity (I conclude)"; of respect: *akṣṇā kāṇaḥ* "blind in one eye"; of space within which, or of the way over or through which a movement takes place: *ādiṣṭena mārgeṇa prayayau* "he went away by the designated route" or of the time within which something happens and is brought to conclusion: *māsenānuvāko 'dhītaḥ* "the section was learned in a month", or also of the time during which an action happens: *tena kālena* "at this time".

IV. THE DATIVE is the "to- and for-case": *mahyaṃ pustakaṃ dehi* "give me the book"; *vanāya pratiṣṭhati* "he sets out for the forest", thus is used especially with verbs of giving, etc., of telling, promising, etc., of wishing, etc., further with verbs denoting anger, acquiescence, etc. The final dative designates the object of striving, purpose, and intention: *phalebhyo gacchati* "he goes out after fruits", *kuṇḍalāya hiraṇyam* "gold for a ring"; *laghūnām api saṃśrayo rakṣāyai bhavati* "even association with the weak is conducive to protection".

V. THE ABLATIVE designates the point of departure; it is the "whence" case: *vanād āgacchati* "he is coming from the forest", *mac chrutvā* (from *mat śrutvā*) "having heard from me", *tad yācitaṃ bhūpāt* "this is requested by the prince", *lobhāt krodhaḥ prabhavati* "anger arises from greed"; also with verbs of desistance, cessation, etc.: *virama karmaṇo 'smāt* "refrain from this action"; of deprivation: *cyutaḥ svarājyāt* "having been deprived of his wealth"; likewise that from which one refrains, against which one defends himself, of which one is afraid, etc.: *caurebhyo rakṣitam* "protected against thieves". This case also designates origin: *brāhmaṇāj jātaḥ* "he was born of a Brahman", reason or cause: *bhayād idam abravīt* "he said this from fear"; frequently of abstracts in *tva,* where we use a clause with "because": *sarvaṃ nityaṃ prameyatvāt* "everything is eternal because it can be imagined". Furthermore, in the abl. is expressed the point from which a distance is reckoned: *tasmāt tṛtīyaḥ* "the third from him"; with comparatives and with words with the meaning "other, different, better (than)" and with other comparative expressions: *dhanyataras tasmād* "more fortunate than he", *mitrād anyaḥ* "other than a friend"; all adjectives can even stand also in the positive with this abl. of comparison: *bhāryā sarvalokād api vallabhā* "the wife is dearer than the whole world".

VI. GENITIVE. Possessive genitive: *nṛpasya senā* "the army of the prince", partitive genitive: *dūraṃ pathaḥ* "a wide stretch of road", objective genitive: *kanyāyāḥ śokaḥ* "grief for a maiden", etc. The genitive of the personal pronoun is used where we as a rule use a possessive pronoun: *mama pitā* "my father"; but there are also poss. pronouns: *madīya-* "mine", etc.; they are not very frequent. It is used with verbs of giving and imparting, of rejoicing in, with "remember", etc.; very often the genitive is used with verbs where we should expect the dative: *dehi valkalaṃ mama* "give me a garment made of bast", *tasya brūyāt sadā priyam* "let him always speak kindly to him"; *hitaṃ tasya* "good for him". Gerundives and the verbal adjectives in *ta* and *na* are often combined with a subjective genitive: *bhartā tava neyaḥ* "your husband should be carried off by you". Many adjectives take this case: full, skilled, able, etc.: *dhanasya pūrṇam* "full of treasures", *tava priyaḥ* "dear to you". There is a genitive absolute (cf. the locative absolute, s. below), which is less frequent than the locative absolute; it is very often concessive: *paśyatas te mariṣyāmi* "although you see it (i.e., before your eyes), I shall die"; the subject is almost always a person, the predicate very often a pres. part. A semi-absolute genitive is also frequently found: *evaṃ tu vartamānasya tasya . . . agamat kālaḥ* "for him who acted in this way, the time came" or "while he . . .".

VII. Locative. This case can be translated in English by "in, at, by, under, on"; it designates place and time, and is used in the real and figurative sense: *pādayoḥ patati* "he falls at the feet of", *ṣaṣṭhe varṣe* "in the sixth year"; *bhṛtyeṣu viśvasan* "putting his trust in his servants"; it is employed with verbs of giving, sending, etc. often as the "whither" case: *brāhmaṇeṣu dattam* "it is given to Brahmans"; it designates 'in which respect": *adhiko bale* "superior in strength", "in regard to which purpose": *carmaṇi dvīpinaṃ hanti* "he kills the panther for the sake of its skin"; it is used with adj. which mean "experienced, etc.": *yuddhe kuśalaḥ* "experienced in war". The locative absolute, i.e., a locative of a noun connected with that of a participle, which designates an external circumstance preceding or accompanying the action of the sentence, is very frequent. This construction can be translated in English by temporal, causal, concessive, and conditional dependent clauses: *mūle hate hataṃ sarvam* "if the root is killed, then everything is killed"; *na rājānaṃ vinā rājyaṃ balavatsv api mantriṣu* "a kingdom does not exist without a king even if (or: although) the ministers are powerful"; *varṣaśate pūrṇe muniḥ Sagarāya varaṃ prādāt* "when the century was complete, the ascetic granted a wish to Sagara". Sometimes the subject remains undesignated: *varṣati* "if it rains", *tathānuṣṭhite* "when such had happened".

VIII. THE PLURAL of the name of a people designates countries and regions: *Madrāḥ* "the land of the Madra".

§ 115. TENSES AND MOODS.

I. THE PRES. INDICATIVE designates actions which take place in the present, ever-valid events, continuing, not completed actions. To presents of duration *sma* can be added; in older times such pres. with *sma* designated duration in the past: *tatra sma rājate Bhaimī* "there was resplendent Bhīma's daughter (and indeed as was her custom)"; later careless use is encountered also: pres. with *sma* can also indicate the past in general: *kasmiṃścin nagare brāhmaṇaḥ prativasati sma* "in a city there lived a Brahman". The present without *sma* can designate duration in the past if misunderstanding is precluded. The near future can also be expressed by the present: *kathāṃ kathayāmi* "I want to tell a story". *ās-* "sit", *sthā-* "stand", and other verbs can express an action in progress especially with a pres. part.

II. Tenses of the past. The AORIST in Vedic designates the current past, the imperfect events which have lost their currentness: "Yama died, (then the gods came and asked his sister Yamī; she answered): he has died today": *yamo vā amriyata* (impf.) . . . *abravīd adyāmṛteti* (*amṛta* aor. + *iti*). The PERFECT designates in the oldest texts the action which has come to a conclusion in the present. In Sanskrit the impf. always has historical meaning, the perf. almost always has it, and the aorist, which is not frequent in all types of literature, is often simply a tense of the past. Very often PRETERITAL PARTICIPLES (§ 102) are also used as finite verbs of the past: *rājā mṛtaḥ* "the king died", *Yamaḥ prayātaḥ* "Y. set out on the road"; *vayaṃ rākṣasān dṛṣṭavantaḥ* (§ 103) "we have seen Rākṣasas"; a form of *bhū-* "become", etc. can also be added: *gatābhūt* "she has, had gone"; also passive: *tena . . . āyātam* (§ 114 III) "he came". In post-Vedic times the *ta-* and *na-* verbal adjectives often continue to fulfill the function of the aorist.

III. THE OPTATIVE expresses a) a wish or request: *tasyā rudhiraṃ pibeyam* "I should like to drink her blood" (often with *api*), *gaccheḥ* "please go", b) a possibility:

kadācid gośabdena budhyeta "he should perhaps awaken owing to the lowing of the cows"; *kathaṃ vidyāṃ Nalam?* "how would I be able to recognize Nala?"; doubt: *taṃ hanyād bāṇaḥ* "will the arrow (be able to) kill him?" c) an hypothesis: *yadi syāt pāvakaḥ śītaḥ* "if fire were cold . . . "; it stands d) in final and consecutive clauses: *tathā prayatnam ātiṣṭhed yathātmānaṃ na pīḍayet* "may he take pains so that he may not worry". e) in relative clauses of general content: *yo* + opt., "if anyone . . ." and in other cases; in several texts it is as a rule prescriptive: *śūdraṃ kārayed dāsyam* "may he let a Śūdra be subservient", especially in later texts (but already in the epics and earlier) it is frequently to be translated by a pres. indic. with or even without "perhaps".

IV. In post-Vedic texts the PERIPHRASTIC FUTURE as a rule designates actions which may be expected at a definite moment, often in curses, promises, etc.

V. IMPERATIVE. This mood can also express a wish: *imāṃ mahīṃ rājā praśāstu naḥ* "may our king rule over this earth"; *ciraṃ jīva* "live long"; it often has (especially in the 1st person) dubitative or potential meaning: *kathaṃ mocyāmahai* "how can we be saved?". The passive imperative is often used as a polite form: *gamyatām* "one should depart; go, please". A frequent polite form is also *arhati* + inf.: *māṃ tyaktum arhasi* "they should, are to leave me". Although *mā* + imp. also occurs (polite *na* + *arhasi*: *na māṃ tyaktum arhasi*), as a rule the augmentless aorist with *mā* (§ 82) is expression of a prohibition: *mā bhaiḥ* "do not be afraid".

§ 116. OTHER VERBAL FORMS.

I. PASSIVE. In the post-Vedic language the use of the passive expression even increases: *tulā mūṣikair bhakṣitā* "the balance is eaten up by the mice", i.e., "the mice have eaten up the balance"; *pṛṣṭaś ca śreṣṭhinā* "the master of the guild asked him". The passive is frequently intransitive: *dṛśyate* "he appears", *yavaḥ pacyate* "the barley becomes ripe".

II. CAUSATIVE. This form expresses the causing, ordering, effecting of an action: *Devadattaḥ svapiti* "D. sleeps", *Devadattaṃ svāpayāmi* "I put D. to sleep"; *vāṇijyaṃ nṛpaḥ kārayed vaiśyam* "the prince should let a Vaiśya carry on trade"; in the passive: *vaiśyo nṛpeṇa vāṇijyaṃ kāryate.*

III. DESIDERATIVE. The desiderative designates the action as desired, intended: *jijñāsate* (*-ti*) "he wishes to become acquainted with", also as imminent: *mumūrṣati* "he is about to die, on the point of dying, faces death". Beside the d. an adj. in *u* can stand from the d.-stem: *mumūrṣu-* "desiring to die, on the point of dying, about to die", and likewise a subst. in *ā*: *mumūrṣā-* "the desire to die, etc.". Some very common d. have almost become independent verbs: *pipāsati* "be thirsty" from *pā-* (*pibati*) "drink".

IV. INTENSIVE. The int. expresses that the action happens emphatically or often: *pepīyate* (cf. § 100) "drink greedily or repeatedly" from *pā-* "drink".

V. VERBAL ADJ. IN *-ta* AND *-na* (perf. pass. part.) and the *tavant-* forms s. above §§ 102 and 103. Periphrastic construction: *śrutaṃ tena tad abhūt* "that had been heard by him". The pres. part. with *ās-* "sit", *sthā-* "stand", and other verbs is used to express an uninterrupted action in progress: *eṣo 'nayā krīḍann* (§ 12 III) *āsta* Eng. "he was sporting with her".

VI. THE INFINITIVE is dependent on verbs and adjectives which express a beginning, striving, or undertaking; a capability or ability; a going, wishing, desiring, having to, deserving, etc. It designates the objective or purpose of an action. Examples: *saṃkhyātum ārabdhaḥ* "having begun to count", *pratyākhyātuṃ na mārhasi* "do not reject me". The infinitive is in itself neither active nor passive. It can be made dependent on a passive verb or verbal adjective or on an adjective with passive meaning; we translate by means of the passive infinitive with an active finite verb: *nāhartuṃ śakyate* "it cannot be produced"; *pitā te mārayituṃ nīyate* "your father is led there in order to be killed". An inf. is often dependent on the gerundive *śakya-*: a) *śakya-* is adj.: *na durvṛttaiḥ śakyo draṣṭuṃ maheśvaraḥ* "the great lord (god) cannot be seen by villains", b) *śakyam* is indeclinable: *doṣo na śakyam ativartitum* "(he) cannot escape from this infirmity"; cf. also *yuktā pariṇetuṃ mama* "she is suited to be married by me".

VII. THE GERUNDIVES (participles of necessity) express a necessity, possibility, obligation, etc. They can be used as predicate and as attribute to a subst. and have the same case, gender, and number as the subst. The agent stands in the instrumental or genitive. They can also be used impersonally and then appear in the nom. sg. of the neuter. Examples: *kasmai kanyā deyā* "to whom should the girl be given?"; *tvayātra bhojanaṃ kāryam* "here you should prepare the food", *bhartā te mayā muktas, tava neyaḥ* "your husband is freed by me, you can take him along";

atra bhavitavyam anayā "here she must stay"; *na bhetavyam* "do not be afraid". In addition to the agent of an impers. grdv. an attribute of the agent defining the sentence predicate can occur: *tvayā prahṛṣṭayā bhāvyam* "you should be happy".

§ 117. The absolutive (gerund) has the character of an indeclinable aorist participle; it stands almost always in conjunction with a noun or pronoun in the sentence, which can be treated as subject of the gerund; this is as a rule the logical or also the grammatical subject of the whole sentence: *tam abravīt prahasyendraḥ* "Indra spoke to him after he (I). had burst out laughing (bursting out laughing)"; *gatvā śīghram ācakṣva* "after you have gone, report quickly", i.e., "go and report . . ."; *sandhyām anvāsta Nalo 'kṛtvā pādayoḥ śaucam* "Nala performed vespers without having washed his feet"; *mantribhir militvā Damayantī vijñaptā* "after the ministers had assembled, D. was informed by them"; *piṭhikām ārūḍho dṛṣṭvaiva dāsībhir āśu rajjūtkṣipto gavākṣeṇa praviveśa* "after he had climbed onto the little bench, he was pulled up with the rope by the female servants as soon as they had seen him, and stepped in through the window". The gerund with *api* is concessive. Some gerunds have the value of prepositions: *uddiśya* approximately = *prati*, *muktvā* (*muc-*), *vihāya* (*hā-*), etc. "without", *ādāya* "with".

§ 118. Sentence structure. A very frequent conjunction is *yad* (*yat*). It introduces a clause of content, i.e., a clause which explains or paraphrases the contents of a part of the main sentence: *itaḥ kaṣṭataraṃ kiṃ tu yad vayaṃ gahane vane gantuṃ na śaknumaḥ* "what is worse than this, that we cannot walk in the impenetrable forest". After a verb of saying, thinking, etc. *yad* often introduces a dependent clause to paraphrase the object: *vedmi yat prāṇo brahma* "I know that the breath is the Brahma". *yad* can mean "inasmuch as, as" and even have the meaning of the causal "because"; *tasmād, tena,* etc. are correlative with it: *yat tvayā pūjito 'smi, tataḥ prīto 'smi* "because you have honored me, therefore I am satisfied". *yad* can also have final and other meanings.

Yāvat, combined with *na* "not", means "before": *yāvat tava vināśo na bhavati, tāvad gaccha* "before your destruction occurs, go".

§ 119. Direct discourse; *iti.* Direct discourse is very common in Sanskrit; it is as a rule designated by addition of the particle *iti*: *sā brūhīti pitrā saṃcoditā* "she was incited by her father with the word 'speak' ". *iti* can also stand alone without verb at the end of a quoted speech; one must here add a verb of saying, judging, thinking, promising, etc.; *iti* is to be translated in a literary translation by our quotation marks: *samidhaḥ kurvata* (§ 7) *edho 'sīti* "one prepares for himself pieces of firewood (reciting the formula): 'you are firewood' ". In this way is paraphrased the object which depends on words expressing a mental or sensual activity, etc.: *devo 'yam iti manyamānaḥ* "believing, this is a god", i.e., "believing that this is a god". In the same use we also find *iti* alone: *vane toyam iti prādhāvat* "in the belief that there was water in the forest, he ran away". Elsewhere one can translate *iti* by "so that": *mā bhūd āśramapīḍeti parimeya-puraḥsarau* "they had only a small retinue so that the hermitage would not be disturbed", or by: "because, for this reason" (*iti kṛtvā*): *sakheti kṛtvā pṛṣṭo vakṣyāmy ahaṃ tvayā* "since you are my friend, I shall say what was asked by you"; or by "like": *tvam ambayā putra iti pratigṛhītaḥ* "you have been received by my mother like a son". The word also serves to designate individual words, mainly proper names as predicative designations of another noun in the sentence. The word before *iti* is then in the nominative: *Sāvitrīti nāmāsyāś cakruḥ* "they called her S.", *rājarṣir iti māṃ viduḥ* "one knows that I am a rājarṣi"; *bubudhe vikṛteti tām* "he observed that she had changed". *Dilīpa iti rājā* means "a king named Dilīpa".

EXERCISES

I

§ 21

1. āsīn Madreṣu pārthivo dakṣaḥ. 2. ācāraḥ pradhāno dharmaḥ. 3. yatra yatra dhūmas, tatra tatra pāvakaḥ. 4. yatra vanaṃ tatra vṛkṣāḥ. 5. yathā vṛkṣas tathā phalam. 6. brāhmaṇaḥ Sagarāya varaṃ prādāt. 7. kaccid dṛṣṭo vane dāruṇe Nalaḥ? 8. duḥkhaṃ kadācit sukhasya mūlam. 9. vyāghro vyādhasya bāṇena hataḥ. 10. upadeśo mūrkhāṇām asakṛt prakopāya. 11. nagaraṃ Rāmasya putreṇa jitam. 12. nṛpo muditaḥ svam eva bhavanaṃ yayau. 13. aputrasya gṛhaṃ śūnyam. 14. naraḥ sarpeṇa daṣṭo na jīvati. 15. anviccha brāhmaṇaṃ guṇair upetam. 16. deva uvāca Madrāṇāṃ pārthivam iṣṭaṃ vacanam. 17. mūṣikāḥ śyenena bhakṣitāḥ. 18. śīlaṃ narasya bhūṣaṇam. 19. pārthiva brāhmaṇasya putrā vyāghreṇa hatāḥ. 20. grāmān nagaraṃ jagāma. 21. na tathā svagṛhe, mitra, yathā tava gṛhe sadā.

---

1 — āsīn = āsīt (§ 10) "(he) was". Madreṣu: § 114, VII. pārthivo: § 15; dakṣaḥ: § 4 VI.
3 — yatra yatra "wherever".
6 — prādāt: 3rd sg. aor. act. pra + dā- "give".
10 — prakopāya: § 114 IV; ṇ: § 20 I.
11 — putreṇa: § 20 I.
12 — yayau: 3rd sg. perf. yā- "go".
14 — na jīvati "does not live", i.e. "will die".
15 — anviccha: 2nd sg. pres. act. imper. anu-iṣ- "seek".
16 — uvāca: 3rd sg. perf. act. vac- "speak" § 114 II.
20 — jagāma: 3rd sg. perf. act. gam- "go".
21 — sva-gṛhe "own house"; tava, § 47, gen. sg. tvam "you".

II

§ 22

1. Bhīmasya sutā dīnā bhavati. 2. sarpeṇa daṣṭā kanyā mṛtā. 3. bhadre, nṛpasya senayā ripu-senā jitā. 4. lajjayā kanyā na pratyabhāṣata. 5. Sītayā ıahito Rāmo 'tiduḥkhito 'bhavat. 6. kanyābhiḥ phalāni dattāni. 7. kanyāyai phalaṃ prādāt. 8. bhadre, śālāyāṃ kanyāḥ sīdanti. 9. kṛpayā dhanaṃ prādāt. 10. kanyayoḥ preṣyā śālāṃ jagāma. 11. Sītayā kanyāyai phalaṃ dattam. 12. bhāryayā sahito Rāmo jagāma.

1 — bhavati: 3rd sg. pres. act. ind. bhū- "become, be".
2 — mṛtā: § 115 II.
3 — ripu-senā "army of the enemy". jitā: § 115 II.
4 — pratyabhāṣata: 3rd sg. impf. mid. prati-bhāṣ- "answer".
5 — 'bhavat: 3rd sg. impf. act. bhū- s. l; § 7.
8 — sīdanti "they sit": § 61 V.

III

§ 23

1. paśor duḥkhena sādhur duḥkhito bhavati. 2. śatrau sāntvaṃ pratīkāraḥ. 3. dharmeṇa hīnāḥ paśubhiḥ samānāḥ. 4. patyuḥ sakhye paśūn dehi. 5. agnir evāgner bheṣajam. 6. guror gṛhaṃ jagāma. 7. śatro mā jahi bhūpatim. 8. arīñ jahi sakhe. 9. Hareḥ kanyāṃ Rāmaḥ pariṇayati. 10. Viṣṇoḥ Śivasya ca bhārye gate. 11. chāyāyām avayas tiṣṭhanti. 12. gurū śiṣyayoḥ krudhyataḥ. 13. paraśunā vṛkṣān kṛntati. 14 bālo gurave phalaṃ prādāt.

1 — bhavati: 3rd sg. pres. act. ind. bhū- "become".
4 — dehi: 2nd sg. pres. act. imperative dā- "give".
7 — mā "not" (with the imperative). jahi: 2nd sg. pres. act. imp. han- "kill".
9 — pariṇayati: 3rd sg. pres. act. ind. pari-nī- "marries".
11 — tiṣṭhanti: 3rd pl. pres. act. ind. sthā- "stand".
12 — krudhyataḥ: 3rd du. pres. act. ind. krudh- "be angry".
13 — kṛntati: 3rd sg. pres. act. ind. kṛt- "cut".

IV

§§ 24-26

1. upadeśo mūrkhāṇāṃ na śāntaye. 2. dhenvai śādvalaṃ dehi. 3. vāriṇā śucinā pāṇī prakṣālaya. 4. sarvā gatīr jagāma. 5. vṛthā vṛṣṭiḥ samudrasya. 6. dhenuṃ mā jahi. 7. madhu vāriṇo madhutaram. 8. vāriṇi haṃsāḥ plavante. 9. dheno kṣīraṃ dehi. 10. dhenūr dehi munaye.

1 — śāntaye: § 114 IV.
3 — prakṣālaya: 2nd sg. pres. act. imp. ksal- with pra "wash off".
4 — sarvā: acc. pl. fem.
5 — samudrasya: gen. instead of dat.
7 — madhutara- "sweeter": §§ 46; 114 V.
8 — plavante "they swim".

V

§§ 27-28

1 na nāryo vinerṣyayā. 2. striyo nisargād eva paṇḍitāḥ. 3. nadyāṃ haṃsaḥ plavate. 4. strīṃ paśya. 5. vadhvai mahatīm ajāṃ dehi. 6. bhuvo nadīṣu matsyāḥ santi. 7. dāsībhyāṃ bhikṣāṃ dehi. 8. vadhvā bālo dhātryai dattaḥ. 9. strī balinī dhātrībhyāṃ dṛṣṭā. 10. nadyos tīreṣu vadhva āsate. 11. nṛpatir nagarīṃ senayājayat. 12. devīr devāṃś ca pūjayati. 13. nadīṣu matsyān apaśyāma. 14. nagaryā gṛheṣu dhenavo na tiṣṭhanti. 15. patnībhiḥ sahitā nagarīm agacchan.

3 — 3rd sg. pres. act. ind. plu- "swim".
4 — paśya: 2nd sg. pres. act. imper. paś- "see".
6 — santi "they are".
10 — āsate "they sit".
11 — § 5 I. ajayat: 3rd sg. act. impf. ji- "triumph, conquer".
12 — pūjayati: 3rd sg. pr. act. ind. (§ 98) "revere".
13 — apaśyāma: 1st pl. impf. act. paś- "see".
14 — tiṣṭhanti, s. exercise III, 11.
15 — agacchan: 3rd pl. impf. act. gam- "go".

VI

§§ 23-30

1. bhartā paraṃ nāryā bhūṣaṇam. 2. nagaryāṃ Puṣkarāvatyāṃ mama svasā Śrutasenasya bhrātrā pariṇītā. 3. nārī bhartuḥ samīpam agacchat. 4. amṛtaṃ durlabhaṃ nṝṇām. 5. saṃpatteś ca vipatteś ca daivam eva kāraṇam. 6. śatror api guṇān vaded doṣāṃś ca guror api. 7. kanyā sakhībhiḥ sārdhaṃ krīḍantī prasuptam ahiṃ nāpaśyat; ahinā daṣṭā bhuvi papāta. 8. kauliko rātrau samāyāto rājaputryoktaḥ: tvayi jāmātari sthite śatrubhir jito me pitā.

9. arthāturāṇāṃ na sukhaṃ na bandhuḥ
kāmāturāṇāṃ na bhayaṃ na lajjā
vidyāturāṇāṃ na sukhaṃ na nidrā
kṣudhāturāṇāṃ na rucir na pakvam.

---

2 — mama: gen sg. of aham "I". pariṇītā: perf. pass. part. of nī- with the prep. pari (§ 20 I).
3 — agacchat: 3rd sg. impf. act. gam- "go".
6 — vaded: 3rd sg. opt. act. vad- "say": "one should say". doṣāṃś § 12 II.
7 — krīḍantī: pres. act. part. fem. krīḍ- "play". nāpaśyat: § 5 I: 3rd sg. impf. act. paś- "see". papāta: 3rd sg. perf. act. pat- "fall".
8 — samāyāta- "come (together)". °putryā + uktaḥ, § 5 II, uktaḥ "addressed". tvayi j. sthite: loc. abs. § 114 VII. tvayi: loc. of "you": § 47. me "of me" (gen. sg.).
9 — arthāturāṇāṃ: § 110.

VII

§§ 32-35

1. na bhiṣak prabhur āyuṣaḥ. 2. vāyur ambhasi nāvaṃ

---

2 — nāvam § 31. harati: 3rd sg. pres. act. ind. hṛ- "steal, overpower, take away".

harati. 3. dhanī vaṇiṅ nirdhanasya śreṣṭhino duhitaraṃ pariṇayati. 4. tatra nadyaḥ puṇyāḥ puṇyāni ca sarāṃsi. 5. na jalaukasām aṅge jalaukā lagati. 6. Damayantī tu rūpeṇa vapuṣā ca lokeṣu yaśaḥ prāpa. 7. marud ambhasi pakṣiṇaṃ harati. 8. yathā cittaṃ tathā vācaḥ. 9. svargo brahmavidbhyas tṛṇam. 10. havīṃṣi devebhyo dehi. 11. vaṇijaḥ sutā vipady āpannā. 12. vṛddho vaṇig dviṣo duhitaraṃ paryaṇayat. 13. naraḥ sumanā dviṣam apaśyat. 14. cakṣuṣā paśyati mānuṣaḥ.

3 — dhanī: nom. sg. (§ 41). vaṇiṅ: § 10. pariṇayati (nī-): "he marries".
5 — jalaukā: § 34 II. lagati: "he adheres to".
6 — prāpa: 3rd sg. perf. act. āp- with pra "attain".
12 — paryaṇayat "he married".
13 — apaśyat: "(he) saw", cf. 14.
14 — paśyati: 3rd sg. pres. act. ind. paś- "see".

VIII

§§ 36-41

1. rājovāca duhitaraṃ ca vṛddhāṃś ca mantriṇaḥ: kuto gatā bhavantaḥ? 2. ājagāma punar veśma Sāvitrī saha mantribhiḥ. 3. dvīpinaṃ bāṇena hanti. 4. āsīd rājā Nalo nāma. 5. pūrvaṃ hi sakhā me 'si saṃbandhī ca. 6. tasya rājñaḥ putro Vīrasena ity āsīt. 7. yogī rājñaḥ phalaṃ dadau. 8. Nalo dāvaṃ dahyantaṃ mahāntaṃ dadarśa. 9. vidvadbhir balibhiḥ

1 — gatā: § 115 II. uvāca "he spoke".
2 — ājagāma punar "(he, she) came back". veśma: acc. of destination § 114 II.
3 — hanti: 3rd sg. pres. act. ind. han- "kill".
4 — āsīd: No. I, 1.
5 — sakhā-, s. sakhi-. 'si: 2nd sg. pres. ind. as- "be".
6 — iti: § 119, tasya: § 48.
7 — rājñaḥ: gen. instead of dat. dadau: "(he) gave".
8 — dahyantaṃ "burning"; dadarśa "(he) saw".
9 — § 14.

sumanobhī rājabhiḥ prajāḥ su-rakṣitāḥ. 10. rājño gṛhe bhiṣag āsīt. 11. vaṇijaḥ sutā rājñā pariṇītā. 12 tyāgo guṇo vittavatām. 13. duḥsparśaḥ pāṇinā śikhī. 14. na rājānaṃ vinā rājyaṃ balavatsv api mantriṣu. 15. balavate rājñe dhīmantau mantriṇau dehi.

16. vāṇī sārasvatī yasya bhāryā rūpavatī satī
Lakṣmīr dānavatī yasya, saphalaṃ tasya jīvitam.

---

10 — āsīt "he was".
11 — pariṇītā "(was) married".
16 — yasya (§ 50): gen. instead of dat. satī: nom. sg. fem. pr. part. as- "be", also "good". tasya: gen. instead of dat.

IX

§§ 47-49

1. anayor aśvayoḥ svāmy ayaṃ naraḥ 2. mahyam eṣā gaur dattā, na tubhyam. 3. ime narā dhaninaḥ santi. 4. dinād dinaṃ gacchaty asmākaṃ yauvanam. 5. āvābhyāṃ dhanaṃ dehi. 6. yuvayor mitreṇāsmad gaur hṛtā. 7. yuṣmadbhrātā dhanī. 8. asmatsvasā nārī sundarī. 9. tāsu nārīṣv etena nareṇemāni vacāṃsy uktāni. 10. asyāṃ puryāṃ bahavo narāḥ santi. 11. asyai vadhvai gṛhaṃ dehi. 12. matpitā vṛddho 'sti.

---

3 — santi "they are".
4 — gacchati: 3rd sg. pres. act. ind. gam- "go (away)".
6 — § 51.
7 — § 110.
12 — 'sti: 3rd sg. pres. ind. as- "be".

X

§§ 53-56

1. viṃśatir nārīṇāṃ mṛtā. 2. idaṃ gṛhaṃ rūpakāṇāṃ śatena gṛhītam. 3. prathame varṣe rājā mṛtaḥ. 4. vaṇijo

---

2 — gṛhītam: i.e. "bought".
4 — samāgatāḥ "(they have) come (together)".

duhitur arthe catvāro varāḥ samāgatāḥ. 5. tṛtīye varṣe yuddham abhavat. 6. saptame loke Brahmā vasati. 7. ṣaḍ doṣāḥ puruṣeṇa hātavyāḥ. 8. dvābhyām aśvābhyāṃ ṣaṣṭhe divase daśame muhūrte jagāma. 9. trayo 'śvāś caturbhyo brāhmaṇebhyo dattāḥ. 10. aṣṭābhir vīraiś catasṛbhyo vadhūbhyas trīṇi sahasrāṇi phalānāṃ dattāni.

XI

§§ 46-56

1. kasmiṃścin nagare dvau brāhmaṇau vasataḥ. 2. kā sā nārī? 3. svāmin, vañcitā vayam anena durjanena. 4. tasminn antarhite nāge prayayau Nalaḥ. 5. kasya nārīyam asti? 6. na bhavati tvad dhanyataraḥ. 7. ete trayaḥ puruṣasya gariṣṭhā bhavanti: ācāryaḥ pitā mātā ca. 8. siddhāḥ sarve yuṣmākaṃ manorathāḥ. 9. kaiṣā purī? 10. asminn eva gṛhe so 'bhavat. 11. keṣu gṛheṣu tvam abhavaḥ? 12. sarvasyātithir guruḥ. 13. yasya gṛhe bhāryā nāsti, tenāraṇyaṃ gantavyam. 14. bho bhavantaḥ sarve mūrkhatamāḥ. 15. tena mūrkheṇa nareṇa khaḍgo gṛhītaḥ. 16. aho kenopāyenaiteṣāṃ dhanaṃ labhe? 17. etan mayā parijñātam.

18. mitradrohī kṛtaghnaś ca yaś ca viśvāsaghātakaḥ
 te narā narakaṃ yānti yāvac candradivākarau.

---

1 — kasmiṃścin: § 10. vasataḥ "they (dual) dwell".
4 — tasminn: § 12. prayayau "(he) went away".
5 — § 5 I.
6 — bhavati "there is..." tvad: § 114 V (abl. comp.).
10 — asminn: § 12 IV. 'bhavat: § 7.
11 — abhavaḥ: 2nd sg. impf. bhū- "become, be".
12 — sarvasya: gen. instead of dat.
13 — tena gantavyam "he should go".
16 — § 5 II. labhe "I get".
17 — etan: § 10.
18 — viśv.: § 110. yānti "they go". candrad.: § 109.

XII

§§ 59-61

1. gardabho na gāyati. 2. mātaraṃ toṣayet. 3. dināḥ kṣipraṃ gacchanti. 4. sarvaṃ lokam apaśyaḥ. 5. śiṣyau bhikṣām ayācetām. 6. Kālidāsaṃ kaviṃ sevāmahe. 7. nīcāḥ kalaham icchanti. 8. kanyā Gaṅgāyās tīre 'krīḍan. 9. kīrtiṃ labhante kavayaḥ. 10. śṛgālau vanād adhāvatām. 11. śilāṃ bharatam. 12. rājānaṃ sevevahi. 13. hastena śilām akṣipat sainikaḥ. 14. siṃhā vanaṃ dhāvantu. 15. bahūni phalāni labhadhvam. 16. Himālayaṃ gacchāva. 17. gṛhaṃ gacchatu. 18. Kāśyām ajāyathāḥ. 19. vadhūṃ labhāmahai. 20. bhāraṃ bhareyāthām. 21. paśya śvānam: tava putram adaśat. 22. brāhmaṇo jalam apibat. 23. tiṣṭhantu bhavantaḥ. 24. atra tiṣṭha. 25. kena jīvāmaḥ?

21 — śvānam: § 40.
25 — jīv- with instr. "live on".

XIII

§§ 59-61

1. tatra tāṃ rajanīm avasāmahi. 2. putrā me bahavo devi bhaveyuḥ. 3. anviccha bhartāraṃ guṇavantam. 4. nadītīre tapasvī tiṣṭhati. 5. tad enaṃ pṛcchāvaḥ. 6. Jahnuḥ kruddho jalaṃ sarvaṃ Gaṅgāyā apibat. 7. yasmiñ jīvati jīvanti bahavaḥ so 'tra jīvatu. 8. nocchritaṃ sahate kaścit. 9. śrīḥ kīrtiś ceha vasetām. 10. sasyāni mahītale roheyuḥ. 11. dhīro

3 — anviccha: iṣ- with anu, § 61 I.
4 — tiṣṭhati: § 61 V.
6 — Gaṅgāyā: § 15. apibat: § 61 V.
7 — y. j.: loc. abs.: § 114 VII.
8 — § 5 II.
9 — § 5 II.

nendriyārtheṣu sajate. 12. viśeṣaṃ nādhigacchāmi nirdhanasyāvarasya ca.

13. te dhanyās te vivekajñās te sabhyā iha bhūtale,
āgacchanti gṛhe yeṣāṃ kāryārthaṃ suhṛdo janāḥ.
14. gandhena gāvaḥ paśyanti vedaiḥ paśyanti vai dvijāḥ
cāraiḥ paśyanti rājānaś cakṣurbhyām itare janāḥ.
15. atirūpād gatā Sītā atigarveṇa Rāvaṇaḥ
atidānād Balir baddhaḥ sarvatrātiśayaṃ tyajet.
16. subhāṣitena gītena yuvatīnāṃ ca līlayā
yasya na dravati svāntaṃ, sa vai mugdho 'thavā paśuḥ.

12 — § 5 I.
13 — āg. g. y.: y. g. āg.
15 — gatā "fell".
16 — word order: yasya sv. s. g. y. ca l. na dr., sa, etc.

XIV

§§ 62-64

1. pitaraṃ mā dveṣāvahai. 2. strī rājñaḥ samīpam eti. 3. brāhmaṇaṃ mā dviṣṭa. 4. satyaṃ brūhi. 5. kiṃ rodiṣi? mā rudihi. 6. Gaṅgām itaḥ. 7. asāva dhīrau. 8. Himālayam aima. 9. aśvaṃ hanyuḥ. 10. Śivaḥ pātu tvām. 11. udeti savitā. 12. siṃhaṃ jahi. 13. bahavo brāhmaṇā vane 'sminn āsan. 14. edhi dharmavān. 15. Kāśīm ayāni. 16. rājānaḥ pṛthivīṃ śāsati. 17. gāṃ dugdha. 18. devam astauḥ. 19. bhūmau śerate. 20. Vedam adhīte. 21. śatrum adviṣātām. 22. Gaṅgāyās tīre 'śayi. 23. siṃham aghnan. 24. gṛha āsmahe. 25. bālo 'rodat.

XV

§§ 62-70

1. devaḥ śarma dadātu. 2. tvāṃ na jahiṁaḥ. 3. parān vṛṇīte svān dveṣṭi. 4. brāhmaṇo na pakṣimāṃsaṃ bhuñjīta.

3 — subject: one.

5. mitrāya dehi dhanam. 6. brāhmaṇaḥ pustakaṃ krīṇāti. 7. aṇḍāni bibhrati svāni na bhindanti pipīlikāḥ. 8. Ayodhyām imaḥ. 9. Rudrāya dadhyān manaḥ. 10. adviṣantaṃ kathaṃ dviṣyāt tvādṛśaḥ? 11. nāśvaṃ na rathaṃ jīrṇo bhuṅkte na ca striyam. 12. sa śabdaḥ sarvā diśaḥ samāvṛṇot. 13. devā bruvanti: varaṃ vṛṇīṣva. 14. asyāṃ nadyāṃ snātvā śīghraṃ punīte brāhmaṇaḥ. 15. Durgāṃ dṛṣṭvā kāmam īpsitam avāpnoti. 16. etasminn agnau brāhmaṇā annaṃ juhvati. 17. bravītu me bhavān. 18. vaṇikputraś ciraṃ kālaṃ bhrāntvā punaḥ svapuram āgatya taṃ śreṣṭhinam abravīt: bhoḥ śreṣṭhin, dehi me tāṃ tulām. 19. atimatiṃ tvāṃ hi vākyair anumimīmahe. 20. Lakṣmyai manāṃsi dadhmaḥ. 21. na kūṭair āyudhair hanyāṃ ripūn. 22. vyāghraṃ jahi. 23. yām iṣuṃ haste bibharṣi, śivāṃ tāṃ kuru. 24. pakṣī phalaṃ svādv atti. 25. Rudro no buddhyā śubhayā saṃyunaktu.

26. gṛhaṃ śatrum api prāptaṃ viśvastam akutobhayam
yo hanyāt, tasya pāpaṃ syāc chatabrāhmaṇaghātajam.

27. spṛśann api gajo hanti jighrann api bhujaṃgamaḥ
hasann api nṛpo hanti mānayann api durjanaḥ.

---

9 — dadhyān: § 10.
14 — snātvā "after he has bathed" (§ 106).
15 — § 106.
18 — brāntvā "after he has roamed about". āgatya "after he had come (back)".
19 — vākyair anum. "from the reports . . . that you are of high intelligence".

XVI

§§ 71-83; 107

1. yaśaḥ prāpsyase. 2. yakṣās tatra na prabhaviṣyanti. 3. rājā taṃ nihaniṣyati. 4. tadā tvaṃ mokṣyase śāpāt. 5. gurave phalaṃ dātāsmi. 6. yaḥ ślokaṃ paṭhiṣyati, yo vā śroṣyati, tau

muktau bhaviṣyataḥ. 7. patnīṃ draṣṭāsi. 8. rājā bhikṣum upāgāt. 9. rājā vaktuṃ nājñāsīt. 10. striyai phalāny adāma. 11. nagarīm agāḥ. 12. bālo na vyaraṃsīt. 13. taṃ pustakaṃ tāpaso 'grahīt. 14. nagaram ajeṣṭhāḥ.

---

9 — vaktum: inf. vac- "speak".

XVII

§§ 84-96

1. mantrī bhāryāṃ jagāda. 2. Rāmo bhāryāṃ tatyāja. 3. nṛpo nāvam āruroha. 4. yuvatī gṛhaṃ gantum iyeṣa. 5. nṛpaḥ śavaṃ skandhe jagrāha. 6. śūro raṇe śirāṃsi sainikānāṃ jahāra. 7. sainiko jaṅghāś cicchedāśvānām. 8. rājā grāmaṃ viveśa. 9. Nalo bhāryām upājagāma. 10. śūro na śokenāvasasāda. 11. parārtho yena sādhyate, sa mahāsattva ucyate. 12. nityaṃ muṣyāmahe caurai rātrau rātrau prabho, lakṣyante te ca nāsmābhiḥ. 13. vihagāḥ pāśair badhyante. 14. janair nagaraṃ gamyate. 15. kavibhir nṛpāḥ stūyante. 16. aśvena jalaṃ pīyate. 17. sarpeṇa daśyete narau. 18. naraiḥ kaṭāḥ kriyante. 19. kanyābhyāṃ gītaṃ gīyate. 20. ṛṣir nṛpeṇa dharmaṃ pṛcchyate. 21. vaṇiṅ mātaram abhivādayāṃcakre. 22. he bhārye pakvaṃ peciṣe? 23. yogino mṛgān na vividhuḥ. 24. drumān bhedayāmāsatuḥ. 25. nṛpatī rathaṃ pure bhrāmayāmāsa. 26. ghaṭau jalena pūryete. 27. he śiṣyā guruṇāhūyadhve. 28. phalaṃ pitre dīyate. 29. nagarī nṛpeṇa jīyata iti śrūyate. 30. taṃ deśaṃ māpayāmāsathuḥ.

---

4 — gantum: inf. gam- "go".
12 — rātrau rātrau: iterative or distributive doubling.
24 — iti: § 119.

XVIII

§§ 71-96; 106

1. brūhi kva yāsyasi? 2. tān devān uvācedaṃ vacaḥ: na tatra gamiṣyāmīti. 3. pitā saha kanyayā vanaṃ prayayau. 4. cauro drakṣyaty āmratarum; yadi bhokṣyate tasya phalāni, mariṣyati. 5. tāv aṭamānau nadīm upeyatuḥ. 6. Damayantī suṣvāpa mahītale. 7. gajas taroḥ śākhāṃ puṣkareṇa babhañja. 8. bhikṣur annaṃ khāditvā śeṣāñ jāyāyā ājahāra; sā tān nidadhau. 9. vaṇijo dadṛśur vanaṃ ramyam. 10. vyāyāmenāsya śirasi vedanā jajñe. 11. gamyatām iti mantriṇaḥ preṣayāmāsa. 12. rājāndho babhūva. 13. rājāraṇyaṃ gatas tapas tepe. 14. sakṛt kanyā pradīyate. 15. rājā cauraṃ mocayiṣyati. 16. nṛpāv udvāhaṃ kārayāmāsatuḥ. 17. vidvān sarvatra pūjyate. 18. sā tatra tapasā varṇaṃ manoharaṃ lebhe. 19. tṛṇair vidhīyate rajjur yayā nāgo 'pi badhyate. 20. sā saṃvatsaraṃ proṣya paryetyovāca: katham aśakatarte maj jīvitum iti. 21. caureṇoktam: āvāṃ nagaraṃ moṣiṣyāvaḥ.

22. vṛkṣāṃś chittvā paśūn hatvā kṛtvā rudhirakardamam
yady evaṃ gamyate svarge, narakaṃ kena gamyate?

23. ko 'rthaḥ putreṇa jātena yo na vidvān na dhārmikaḥ?
tayā gavā kiṃ kriyate yā na dogdhrī na garbhiṇī?

---

2 — § 5 I, § 119.
5 — § 101 II.
6 — § 20 II.
8 — khāditvā "after he . . . (khād-)", gerund, § 106.
10 — § 5 I.
12 — § 5 I.
15 — mocayiṣyati: §§ 72; 97.
20 — proṣya: § 106. paryetya: i- "go", with pari and ā; § 106. aśakata ṛte § 5 II. maj: § 11.
22 — svarge: loc. as "whither" case.
23 — putro jātaḥ, the construction of Lat. *urbs condita*: "the birth of a son".

XIX

§§ 97-106

1. Sāvitrī priyavādena bhartāraṃ paryatoṣayat. 2. vāyus tṛṇāni nonmūlayet. 3. puruṣaḥ pradhānaḥ sarvayatnaiḥ parirakṣaṇīyaḥ. 4. dhairyaṃ na tyājyam. 5. tvāṃ Sītāṃ smārayiṣyāmy ahaṃ punaḥ. 6. rājā senāṃ samudraṃ gamayiṣyati. 7. mūḍho 'śocyāni kāryāṇi śocati. 8. sainikā astrāṇi sisṛkṣanti. 9. devān yajñena bhāvayata, te devā bhāvayantu vaḥ. 10. aśvān vāhane yojayantu. 11. hitam ātmanaḥ cikīrṣayeḥ. 12. pāpān nivārayate yojayate hitāya. 13. yajñair devān vardhayeḥ. 14. brāhmaṇaṃ me pitāvāsayat. 15. agnir bhūtāni trāsayann āyāti drumāṃl lelihānaḥ. 16. dadarśa Damayantīṃ dedīpyamānāṃ vapuṣā.

---

2 — § 5 II.
3 — sarvay. = sarvair yatnaiḥ.
5 — constr. with 2 acc., § 114 II.
8 — sṛj-.
14 — § 5 I.

XX

§§ 107-113

1. Pramadvarā gandharvāpsarasoḥ sutāsīt. 2. martyasya nāyur asti gatāyuṣaḥ. 3. adrisamīpe vanam asti. 4. sarpo viṣopaliptān daśanān rājaputryā aṅge nyapātayat. 5. dvijavarā vanavāsinaś cājagmuḥ kṛpānvitāḥ. 6. tatrāsīt saraḥ sumanoharam. 7. Pramadvarāyāṃ sarpadaṣṭāyāṃ mṛtāyāṃ ca Rurur abravīc: chete sā bhuvi tanvaṅgī mama śokavivardhinīti. 8. sa rājā pṛthivīpālaḥ sarvaśastrabhṛtāṃ varo

---

1 — P.: proper name.
7 — P., etc.: loc. abs. chete: § 11. tanvaṅgī: § 22 at the end.

babhūva. 9. rājā mṛgasahasrāṇi hatvā sabalavāhano vanān nirjagāma. 10. sūryo diśam Antakasevitām agacchat. 11. kasmiṃścid vane caṭakadaṃpatī tamālatarukṛtanilayau prativasataḥ sma. 12. hemante Himālayo girir yathārthanāmā himavān asti. 13. brāhmaṇaḥ phalamūlāśano dṛḍhavrataḥ svargaṃ gataḥ. 14. putro guṇānvito mātāpitror hite sadā rataḥ. 15. śatāyuṣaḥ putrapautrān vṛṇīṣva bahūn paśūn hastihiraṇyam aśvān. 16. kāmaṃ vyasanavṛkṣasya mūlaṃ durjanasaṃgatiḥ. 17. dineṣu gateṣu vaṇikputraḥ sukhavismṛtadurgatiḥ svadeśaṃ gantukāmo 'bhūt. 18. abhāryaṃ śūnyaṃ gṛhapater gṛham. 19. tac chrutvā vīkṣituṃ svabhṛtyān preṣya satyam avetya tat sa rājā taṃ vṛddhavaṇijaṃ muktavān. 20. nṛpaḥ sasutābhāryo grāmaṃ prāpa. 21. taṃ muniṃ sūryakarasaṃtāpaklāntaṃ vaṇig dṛṣṭvā kutas tvam iti pṛṣṭavān.

22. yasya cittaṃ dravībhūtaṃ kṛpayā sarvajantuṣu,
tasya jñanaṃ ca mokṣaś ca; kiṃ jaṭābhasmacīvaraiḥ?

23. nāsti kāmasamo vyādhir nāsti mohasamo ripuḥ
nāsti krodhasamo vahnir nāsti jñānasamaṃ sukham.

24. prāvṛṭkāle yātrā yauvanakāle pūruṣadāridryam
prathamasnehe virahaḥ, trīṇy api duḥkhāny atigurūṇi.

25. uttamāḥ svadhanaiḥ khyātāḥ pitṛdravyeṇa madhyamāḥ
adhamā mātulaiḥ khyātāḥ śvāśuraiś cādhamādhamāḥ.

26. na svalpasya kṛte bhūri nāśayen matimān naraḥ,
etad evātipāṇḍityaṃ yat svalpād bhūrināśanam.

---

9 — vanān: § 10.
10 — d. A.: the south.
14 — rataḥ + locative.
15 — ca "and" can be omitted.
22 — kim with instr. "what is the benefit" or "for what purpose".
24 — pūruṣa- = puruṣa- (for the sake of the meter).

READING SELECTIONS

I

Hitop. 2, 5

Asti Śrīparvatamadhye Brahmapurābhidhānaṃ nagaram. tacchailaśikhare [1]) Ghaṇṭākarṇo nāma rākṣasaḥ prativasatīti [2]) janāpavādaḥ sadā śrūyate. ekadā ghaṇṭām ādāya [5]) palāyamānaḥ kaścic cauro vyāghreṇa vyāpāditaḥ khāditaś ca. tatpāṇipatitā ghaṇṭā vānaraiḥ prāptā. te ca vānarās tāṃ ghaṇṭāṃ sarvadaiva vādayanti. tatas tannagarajanaiḥ sa manuṣyaḥ khādito dṛṣṭaḥ. pratikṣaṇaṃ ca ghaṇṭāvādaḥ śrūyate. anantaraṃ Ghaṇṭākarṇaḥ kupito manuṣyān khādati ghaṇṭāṃ ca vādayatīty [3]) uktvā janāḥ sarve nagarāt palāyitāḥ. tataḥ kuṭṭanyā vimṛṣya markaṭā ghaṇṭāṃ vādayantīti svayaṃ parijñāya [4]) rājā vijñāpitaḥ: deva yadi dhanopakṣayaḥ kriyate, tadāham enaṃ Ghaṇṭākarṇaṃ sādhayāmi. tato rājñā dhanaṃ dattam. kuṭṭanyā ca svayaṃ vānarapriyaphalāny ādāya [5]) vanaṃ praviśya phalāny ākīrṇāni. tato ghaṇṭāṃ parityajya vānarāḥ phalāsaktā babhūvuḥ. kuṭṭanī ghaṇṭāṃ gṛhītvā samāyātā sakalalokapūjyābhavat.

---

[1]) sandhi § 11.
[2]) § 119.
[3]) § 119.
[4]) § 117.
[5]) § 106 and § 117 end.

II

Hitop. 3, 3

Asti Hastināpure Viśālo nāma rajakaḥ. tasya gardabho 'tivāhād durbalo mumūrṣur [1]) abhavat. tatas tena rajakenāsau vyāghracarmaṇā pracchādyāraṇyasaṃnidhānasasyamadhye muktaḥ. tato dūrād vyāghrabuddhyā tam avalokya kṣetrapatayaḥ satvaraṃ palāyante. atha kenāpi sasyarakṣakeṇa dhūsarakambalakṛtatanutrāṇena dhanuḥ sajjīkṛtyānatakāyenaikānte [2]) sthitam [3]). taṃ cādūre dṛṣṭvā sa gardabhaḥ puṣṭāṅgo jātabalo gardabhīyam [4]) iti jñātvā śabdaṃ kurvāṇas tadabhimukhaṃ dhāvitaḥ. tatas tena rakṣakeṇa gardabho 'yam iti śabdān niścitya līlayā vyāpāditaḥ.

---

[1]) § 116 III.
[2]) § 5 III.
[3]) i.e., ko 'pi sasyarakṣakaḥ . . . tasthau.
[4]) § 5 I.

III

Pañcatantra 5, 9

Kasmiṃścin nagare kaścit Svabhāvakṛpaṇo nāma brāhmaṇaḥ prativasati sma. tasya bhikṣārjitaiḥ saktubhir bhuktorvaritair ghaṭaḥ paripūritaḥ. taṃ ca ghaṭaṃ nāgadante 'valambya tasyādhastāt khaṭvāṃ nidhāya satatam ekadṛṣṭyā tam avalokayati. atha kadācid rātrau suptaś cintayāmāsa: yat paripūrṇo 'yaṃ ghaṭas tāvat saktubhir vartate, tad yadi durbhikṣaṃ bhavati tad anena rūpakāṇāṃ śatam utpadyate. tatas tena mayājādvayaṃ grahītavyam. tataḥ ṣaṇmāsikaprasavavaśāt tābhyāṃ yūthaṃ bhaviṣyati. tato 'jābhiḥ prabhūtā gā grahīṣyāmi, gobhir mahiṣīr, mahiṣībhir vaḍavāḥ.

vaḍavāprasavataḥ [1]) prabhūtā aśvā bhaviṣyanti. teṣāṃ vikrayāt prabhūtaṃ suvarṇaṃ bhaviṣyati. suvarṇena catuḥśālaṃ gṛhaṃ saṃpadyate. tataḥ kaścid brāhmaṇo mama gṛham āgatya prāptavayaskāṃ [2]) rūpāḍhyāṃ kanyāṃ dāsyati. tatsakāśāt putro me bhaviṣyati. tasyāhaṃ Somaśarmeti [3]) nāma kariṣyāmi. tat tasmiñ jānucalanayogye saṃjāte 'haṃ pustakaṃ gṛhītvāśvaśālāyāḥ pṛṣṭhadeśa upaviṣṭas tad avadhārayiṣyāmi. atrāntare Somaśarmā māṃ dṛṣṭvā jananyutsaṅgāj jānupracalanaparo 'śvakhurāsannavartī matsamīpam āgamiṣyati. tato 'haṃ brāhmaṇīṃ kopāviṣṭo 'bhidhāsyāmi: gṛhāṇa tāvad bālakam. sāpi gṛhakarmavyagratayāsmadvacanaṃ na śroṣyati. tato 'haṃ samutthāya tāṃ pādaprahāreṇa tāḍayiṣyāmi. evaṃ tena dhyānasthitena tathaiva pādaprahāro datto, yathā sa ghaṭo bhagnaḥ. saktubhiḥ pāṇḍuratāṃ gataḥ.

1) § 114 V; -tas forms an abl. sg. from all stems.
2) § 112.
3) § 119.

IV

Pañcatantra 1, 2

Kaścic chṛgālaḥ kṣutkṣāmakaṇṭha itas tataḥ [1]) paribhraman vane sainyadvayasaṃgrāmabhūmim apaśyat. tasyāṃ ca dundubheḥ patitasya vāyuvaśād vallīśākhāgrair hanyamānasya śabdam aśṛṇot. atha kṣubhitahṛdayaś cintayāmāsa: aho vinaṣṭo 'smi. tad yāvan nāsya proccāritaśabdasya dṛṣṭigocare gacchāmi, tāvad anyato vrajāmīti. athavā naitad yujyate sahasaiva pitṛpaitāmahaṃ vanaṃ tyaktum. uktaṃ ca:

bhaye vā yadi vā harṣe saṃprāpte yo vimarśayet [2])
kṛtyaṃ na kurute vegān, na sa saṃtāpam āpnuyāt.

1) itas tataḥ "here and there".
2) yadi . . . yo "if anyone".

tat tāvaj jānāmi kasyāyaṃ śabdaḥ. dhairyam ālambya vimarśayan yāvan mandaṃ mandaṃ pratigacchati, tāvad dundubhim apaśyat. yāvac chākhāgrair vāyuvaśād dhanyate[2]), tāvac chabdaṃ karoti, anyathā tūṣṇīm āste[3]). tataś ca samyak parijñāya samīpaṃ gatvā svayam eva kautukād atāḍayad bhūyaś ca harṣād acintayat: aho cirād etad asmākaṃ mahad bhojanam āpatitam. tan nūnam etan māṃsamedo'sṛgbhiḥ pūritaṃ bhaviṣyati. tataḥ paruṣacarmāvaguṇṭhitaṃ tat katham api vidāryaikadeśe chidraṃ kṛtvā saṃhṛṣṭamanāḥ praviṣṭaḥ. paraṃ carma vidārayato daṃṣṭrābhaṅgaḥ saṃjātaḥ. atha tad dārucarmaviśeṣam ālokya nirāśībhūtaḥ ślokam enam apaṭhat:

pūrvam eva mayā jñātaṃ pūrṇam etad dhi medasā;
yāvat praviśya paśyāmi tāvac carma ca dāru ca.

---

[2]) sandhi! § 17.
[3]) āste, cf. § 115 I.

V

Pañcatantra 1, 13

Asti kasmiṃścij jalāśaye Kambugrīvo nāma kacchapaḥ. tasya Saṃkaṭa-Vikaṭa-nāmnī mitre [1]) haṃsajātīye paramasneham āśrite. tau ca haṃsau sarastīram āsādya tena sahānekadevarṣiṇāṃ kathāḥ kṛtvāstamanavelāyāṃ svanīḍasaṃśrayaṃ kurutaḥ [2]). atha gacchati kāle 'nāvṛṣṭivaśāt saraḥ śanaiḥ śanaiḥ śoṣam agamat. tatas tadduḥkhaduḥkhitau [3]) tāv ūcatuḥ: bho mitra jambālaśeṣam [4]) etat saraḥ saṃjātaṃ. tat

---

[1]) i.e., mitre bhavataḥ.
[2]) saṃśrayaṃ kṛ- "go . . .".
[3]) = tasya duḥkhena duḥkhitau.
[4]) bahuvrīhi, § 112.

kathaṃ bhavān bhaviṣyatīti [5]) vyākulatvaṃ nau [6]) hṛdi vartate. tac chrutvā Kambugrīva āha: bhoḥ sāṃprataṃ nāsty asmākaṃ jīvitavyaṃ jalābhāvāt. tathāpy upāyaś cintyatām iti. uktaṃ ca:

tyājyaṃ na dhairyaṃ vidhure 'pi kāle,
dhairyāt kadācid gatim āpnuyāt saḥ, [7])
yathā samudre 'pi ca potabhaṅge
sāṃyātriko vāñchati tartum [8]) eva.

aparaṃ ca:

mitrārthe bāndhavārthe ca buddhimān yatate sadā
jātāsv āpatsu yatnena, jagādedaṃ vaco Manuḥ.

tad [9]) ānīyatāṃ kācid dṛḍharajjur laghu kāṣṭhaṃ vānviṣyatāṃ ca prabhūtajalasanāthaṃ saro, yena [10]) mayā madhyapradeśe dantair gṛhīte sati [11]) yuvāṃ koṭibhāgayos [12]) tat kāṣṭhaṃ mayā sahitaṃ saṃgṛhya [13]) tat saro nayataḥ. tāv ūcatuḥ: bho mitraivaṃ kariṣyāvaḥ, paraṃ bhavatā maunavratena bhāvyaṃ [14]), no cet tava kāṣṭhāt pāto bhaviṣyati. tathānuṣṭhite gacchatā Kambugrīveṇādhobhāgavyavasthitaṃ kiṃcit puram ālokitam. tatra ye paurās te tathā nīyamānaṃ vilokya savismayam idam ūcuḥ: aho cakrākāraṃ kimapi pakṣibhyāṃ nīyate. paśyata paśyata. atha teṣāṃ kolāhalam

---

5) § 119.
6) § 47.
7) i.e., the man who follows the advice given in line 1.
8) = taritum, inf. of tṝ-, object the sea; he does not remain quietly at home.
9) therefore.
10) so that.
11) mayā with gṛhīte; loc. abs.
12) loc. dual.
13) to yuvām.
14) § 112.

ākarṇya Kambugrīva āha: bhoḥ kim eṣa kolāhala iti vaktumanā ardhokte patitaḥ pauraiḥ khaṇḍaśaḥ kṛtaś ca.

VI

Vetālap.; The Four Suitors

Asti Dharmasthalaṃ nāma nagaram. tatra rājā Guṇādhipo nāma, tatraiva ca Keśavo nāma brāhmaṇo 'sti. tasya duhitā Mandāravatī nāma rūpeṇātīva vikhyātā. sā ca varayogyābhavat. tasyā arthe catvāro varāḥ samāgatāḥ, catvāro 'pi samānaguṇā brāhmaṇāḥ. Keśavaś cintāṃ prapanno babhūva[1]: ekā kanyā, catvāro varāḥ! kasmai deyā? kasmai na deyā? etasminn eva prastāve Keśavasya duhitā kālasarpeṇa daṣṭā tadarthe mantravādinaḥ samānītāḥ. tair mantravādibhis tāṃ vilokya bhaṇitam: kāladaṣṭā[2] na jīvati[3] kanyeyam. mantrivacanaṃ śrutvā tadanantaraṃ brāhmaṇaḥ Keśavo nadītīre gatvā tasyāḥ saṃskāraṃ cakāra. catvāro 'pi varāḥ śmaśāne samāyātāḥ. teṣāṃ madhya[4] ekaś citāyāṃ praviśya mṛtaḥ. dvitīyena tasyā asthīni tadbhasma ca śmaśāne kuṭīrakaṃ kṛtvā rakṣitāni. tṛtīyas tapasvī bhūtvā deśāntaraṃ gataḥ. caturtho nijabhavanaṃ gataḥ.

yo deśāntaraṃ gatas tena deśāntare kasyacid brāhmaṇasya gṛhe gatvā madhyāhne bhojanaṃ prārthitam. gṛhasthena brāhmaṇena bhaṇitam: bhos tapasvin, tvayātraiva bhojanaṃ kāryam. yāvad brāhmaṇyā bhojanaṃ niṣpāditam āsanaṃ ca dattvopaveśitaḥ sa, tāvat tasyā bālakena gṛhe roditum ārabdham. gṛhasthayā brāhmaṇyā sa bālo jvalitāgnau prakṣiptaḥ.

---

1) c.p.b. "he got the thought", i.e., "he reflected".
2) kāladaṣṭā: kālasarpadaṣṭā.
3) na jīvati "will not remain in life".
4) t.m. "among them, of them", a common paraphrase of the partitive genitive.

tad dṛṣṭvā tena bhikṣuṇā calitaṃ, tena brāhmaṇena sa tu nivāritaḥ. tena bhaṇitam: tad dāruṇaṃ karma dṛṣṭvā sahabhojanaṃ na karomi. yasya gṛha īdṛśaṃ rākṣasaṃ karma dṛśyate, tasya gṛhe kathaṃ bhojanaṃ karaṇīyam? tac chrutvā tena gṛhasthena brāhmaṇena gṛhamadhye praviśya pustakam ānītam. tad udghāṭya mantram ekaṃ japitvā bālako bhasmībhūto [5]) jīvāpitaḥ [6]). tapasvinā brāhmaṇasya kautukaṃ dṛṣṭvā cintitam: yadīdaṃ pustakaṃ mama haste ghaṭati, tadāhaṃ tāṃ priyāṃ jīvāpayāmi. iti saṃcintya tatraiva nibhṛto bhūtvā [7]) sthitaḥ [8]). niśīthe gṛhamadhye praviśya tat pustakam apahṛtya tatraiva śmaśāne samāyātaḥ.

yaḥ śmaśāne tiṣṭhati, tena pṛṣṭaḥ: bho mitra, deśāntare gatvā kācid vidyā samājñātā? tenoktam: mṛtasaṃjīvanī vidyā mayā samājñātā. dvitīyenoktam: tarhīmāṃ priyāṃ jīvāpaya. tac chrutvā tena pustakam udghāṭya [9]) mantram ekaṃ japitvā jalena siktvā jīvāpitā kanyā. yaḥ sahaiva mṛtaḥ, so 'pi jīvitaḥ. yo gṛhe gatas, tena śrutvāyātam api [10]). tasyā arthe krodhāndhalocanāc [11]) catvāro 'pi pravivādaṃ kurvanti. — kasya bhāryā bhavati? srūyatām:

yena jīvāpitā kanyā, sa pitā jīvadāyakaḥ;
yaḥ sahaiva mṛtaḥ, so 'pi bhrātā jātaḥ sahaiva yat;
bhasmanāṃ saṃgrahaṃ kṛtvā śmaśāne yena saṃsthitam,
nīcakarmā [12]) sa dāsaḥ syāt; sa bhartā, yo gṛhe gataḥ.

---

5) § 107 II.
6) perf. pass part. of the caus. of jīv- "live".
7) "after he had hidden".
8) cf. § 115 II.
9) § 106.
10) § 115 II: tena . . . āyātam: sa . . . āyayau.
11) i.e., krodhād andhāni locanāni yeṣāṃ te.
12) i.e., nīcaṃ karma yasya saḥ.

VII

Śukasapt. 31

Gurjarajanapade Bhṛgukṣetrābhidhānaṃ nagaram. tatraiko brāhmaṇaḥ. sa tu vaidheyaśakala evātīva daivavirahitaḥ. sa tu devanāya prāvartata. tadanu śanais taskaramatam anvabhavat. tadā kutrāpi khātapatitabhittivibhāge dasyur asau vidhṛtaḥ [1]). rājñaḥ samīpe ninyus tam. rājā pratyādiṣṭavān: corasya daṇḍo bhavati yas, tam etasya kurvantu. yata ūcuḥ: coradaṇḍaḥ śiraśchedaḥ. ity abhidhāya taṃ mārayitum anayat. tadā taskaro rājānaṃ vyajijñapat: deva vijñaptir ekāsti. ahaṃ kimapi cūḍāmaṇisamāhitaṃ jñānam avikalam ākalayāmi. tarhi bhaviṣyataḥ samayasya kamapi jñānaprakāram abhidhāsyāmi. tadanu bhūpālo 'py avadat: vyāharasveti. tato 'sau jagāda: deva etat tvaṃ jānīhi [2]). ekasmāt praharād upari samasto 'pi sargo 'nyathaiva bhaviṣyati. andhakāraḥ pravartiṣyate mahābhayānakaḥ. tarhy evaṃvidhasyātigarīyaso jagadupadravasya śāntikaraṇāya tvayy ākāṅkṣā vartate yadi, tadānīṃ kuru tat. itarathaitat sarvam api parisamāptam evety ahaṃ paśyāmi. tadanu medinīnātho giram asṛjat. tarhy etasyopadravasya kathaṃ śāntir bhavatīty uvāca. tadā rājājñām āsādya so 'py uvāca: tvam eva tasyopadravasya śāntiṃ kariṣyasīty, etadarthe mahyam ātmanaḥ satyavacanaṃ prayaccha, paścād abhidhāsyāmi. tadā rājā tasmai satyavacanaṃ prāyacchat. tato 'sau tacchāntikaṃ rājānam āśrāvayat: madrakṣaṇaṃ kartavyam, etāvatā tacchāntir bhaviṣyatīty avagaccha. rājāpy avocat: anyādṛśī sṛṣṭir bhaviṣyatīti tat kim? [3]) so 'bravīt: avadhatsva mahīmahendra:

---

[1]) § 115 II.

[2]) jñā-.

[3]) iti tat kim: "then what does your assertion mean?"

ātmani praśamite sarvāpi sṛṣṭiḥ samāptarūpaiva. yadāhaṃ mṛtas, tadā samasto 'pi sargo 'nyathā jāta eva. mametareṣām apekṣayā kiṃ nāma prayojanam? tadā rājā tadvacanam apahāsya taṃ niramocayat.

VIII

Mahābhārata 1, 3 beginning

Janamejayaḥ Pārikṣitaḥ saha bhrātṛbhiḥ Kurukṣetre dīrghasattram upāste sma [1]. tasya bhrātaras trayaḥ Śrutasena Ugraseno Bhīmasena iti [2]. teṣu tat sattram upāsīneṣv [3] āgacchat Sārameyaḥ. Janamejayasya bhrātṛbhir abhihato rorūyamāṇo [4] mātuḥ samīpam upāgacchat. taṃ mātā rorūyamāṇam uvāca: kiṃ rodiṣi kenāsy abhihata iti. sa evam ukto mātaraṃ pratyuvāca: Janamejayasya bhrātṛbhir abhihato 'smīti. taṃ mātā pratyuvāca: vyaktaṃ tvayā tatrāparāddhaṃ yenāsyabhihata iti. sa tāṃ punar uvāca: nāparādhyāmi kiṃcin nāvekṣe havīṃṣi nāvaliha [5] iti. tac chrutvā [6] tasya mātā Saramā putraduḥkhārtā tat sattram upāgacchad, yatra sa Janamejayaḥ saha bhrātṛbhir dīrghasattram upāste. sa tayā kruddhayā tatroktaḥ: ayaṃ me putro na kiṃcid aparādhyati nāvekṣate havīṃṣi nāvaleḍhi, kimartham abhihata iti. na kiṃcid uktavantas [7] te. sā tān uvāca: yasmād ayam abhihato 'napakārī, tasmād adṛṣṭaṃ tvāṃ bhayam āgamiṣyatīti. Janamejaya evam ukto devaśunyā Saramayā bhṛśaṃ saṃbhrānto viṣaṇṇaś cāsīt.

---

[1] § 115 I.
[2] § 119.
[3] loc. abs., § 114 VII; § 101 II.
[4] § 100, ru-.
[5] § 7, lih-.
[6] § 11.
[7] § 115 II.

IX

Mbh. 3, 167, 9 ff. (3, 11943 ff.)

Arjuna uvāca:

śṛṇu hanta mahārāja vidhinā yena dṛṣṭavān
Śatakratum ahaṃ devaṃ bhagavantaṃ ca Śaṅkaram.
vidyām adhītya tāṃ rājaṃs tvayoktām arimardana
bhavatā ca samādiṣṭas tapase prasthito vanam.
Bhṛgutuṅgam atho gatvā Kāmyakād āsthitas tapaḥ
ekarātroṣitaḥ kaṃcid apaśyaṃ brāhmaṇaṃ pathi.
sa mām apṛcchat: Kaunteya [1]), kvāsi gantā bravīhi [2]) me.
tasmā avitathaṃ sarvam abruvaṃ Kurunandana.
sa tathyaṃ mama tac chrutvā brāhmaṇo rājasattama
apūjayata māṃ rājan prītimāṃś cābhavan mayi.
tato mām abravīt prītas: tapa ātiṣṭha Bhārata [3]),
tapasyan na cireṇa tvaṃ drakṣyase vibudhādhipam.
tato 'haṃ vacanāt tasya girim āruhya Śaiśiram [4])
tapo 'tapaṃ mahārāja māsaṃ mūlaphalāśanaḥ.
dvitīyaś cāpi me māso jalaṃ bhakṣayato gataḥ,
nirāhāras tṛtīye 'tha māse Pāṇḍavanandana.
ūrdhvabāhuś caturthaṃ tu māsam asmi sthitas tadā
na ca me hīyate prāṇas tad adbhutam ivābhavat [5]).
pañcame tv atha samprāpte prathame divase gate
varāhasaṃsthitaṃ bhūtaṃ matsamīpaṃ samāgamat
nighnan prothena pṛthivīṃ vilikhaṃś caraṇair api
saṃmārjañ jaṭhareṇorvīṃ vivartaṃś ca muhur muhuḥ.

---

[1]) = Arjuna.
[2]) = brūhi.
[3]) = Arjuna.
[4]) = Himālaya.
[5]) It was like a miracle that prāṇo me na hīyate.

anu tasyāparaṃ bhūtaṃ mahat kairātasaṃsthitam
dhanurbāṇāsimat prāptaṃ strīgaṇānugataṃ tadā.
tato 'haṃ dhanur ādāya tathākṣayye maheṣudhī
atāḍayaṃ śareṇātha tad bhūtaṃ lomaharṣaṇam.
yugapat taṃ kirātas tu vikṛṣya balavad dhanuḥ
abhyājaghne dṛḍhataraṃ kampayann iva me manaḥ.
sa tu mām abravīd rājan: mama pūrvaparigrahaḥ
mṛgayādharmam utsṛjya kimarthaṃ tāḍitas tvayā?
eṣa [6]) te niśitair bāṇair darpaṃ hanmi, sthiro bhava.
sa dhanuṣmān mahākāyas tato mām abhyadhāvata,
tato girim ivātyartham avṛṇon māṃ mahāśaraiḥ;
taṃ cāhaṃ śaravarṣeṇa mahatā samavākiram.
tataḥ śarair dīptamukhair yantritair anumantritaiḥ
pratyavidhyam ahaṃ taṃ tu vajrair iva śiloccayam.
tasya tac chatadhā [7]) rūpam abhavac ca sahasradhā,
tāni cāsya śarīrāṇi śaιair aham atāḍayam.
punas tāni śarīrāṇi ekībhūtāni [8]) Bhārata
adṛśyanta mahārāja, tāny ahaṃ vyadhamaṃ punaḥ.
aṇur bṛhacchirā bhūtvā bṛhac cāṇuśirāḥ punaḥ
ekībhūtas tadā rājan so 'bhyavartata māṃ yudhi.
yadābhibhavituṃ bāṇair na ca śaknomi taṃ raṇe
tato mahāstram ātiṣṭhaṃ vāyavyaṃ Bharatarṣabha.
na cainam aśakaṃ hantuṃ tad adbhutam ivābhavat.
tasmin pratihate cāstre vismayo me mahān abhūt.
bhūya eva mahārāja saviśeṣam ahaṃ tataḥ
astrapūgena mahatā raṇe bhūtam avākiram.
tato 'haṃ dhanur ādāya tathākṣayye maheṣudhī

---

6) = aham.
7) sandhi, § 11.
8) § 107.

sahasābhyahanaṃ bhūtaṃ tāny apy astrāṇy abhakṣayat.
hateṣv astreṣu sarveṣu bhakṣiteṣv āyudheṣu ca
mama tasya ca bhūtasya bāhuyuddham avartata.
vyāyāmaṃ muṣṭibhiḥ kṛtvā talair api samāgataiḥ,
apārayaṃś ca tad bhūtaṃ niśceṣṭam agamaṃ mahīm.
tataḥ prahasya tad bhūtaṃ tatraivāntaradhīyata
saha strībhir mahārāja paśyato me 'dbhutopamam.
evaṃ kṛtvā sa bhagavāṃs tato 'nyad rūpam āsthitaḥ
divyam eva mahārāja vasāno 'dbhutam ambaram.
hitvā kirātarūpaṃ ca bhagavāṃs tridaśeśvaraḥ
svarūpaṃ divyam āsthāya tasthau tatra maheśvaraḥ.
adṛśyata tataḥ sākṣād bhagavān Govṛṣadhvajaḥ [9])
Umāsahāyo vyāladhṛg bahurūpaḥ pinākadhṛk.
sa mām abhyetya samare tathaivābhimukhaṃ sthitam
śūlapāṇir athovāca: tuṣṭo 'smīti parantapa,
amaratvam apāhāya brūhi yat te manogatam.
tataḥ prāñjalir evāham astreṣu gatamānasaḥ [10])
praṇamya manasā Śarvaṃ tato vacanam ādade:
bhagavān me prasannaś ced, īpsito 'yaṃ varo mama,
astrāṇīcchāmy ahaṃ jñātuṃ yāni deveṣu kānicit.
dadānīty eva bhagavān abravīt Tryambakaś ca mām,
raudram astraṃ madīyaṃ [11]) tvām upasthāsyati Pāṇḍava.
pradadau ca mama prītaḥ so 'straṃ pāśupataṃ mahat,
uvāca ca mahādevo dattvā me 'straṃ sanātanam:
na prayojyaṃ bhaved etan mānuṣeṣu kathaṃcana,
jagad vinirdahed evam alpatejasi pātitam;

---

[9]) = Śiva.
[10]) astreṣu to be joined with gata°; gatamānasaḥ is a bahuvrihi comp., astreṣu, weapons (i.e., to be obtained).
[11]) § 114 VI.

pīḍyamānena [12]) balavat [13]) prayojyaṃ syād Dhanañjaya.
mūrtiman me sthitaṃ pārśve prasanne Govṛṣadhvaje
utsādanam amitrāṇāṃ parasenānikartanam.
anujñātas tv ahaṃ tena tatraiva samupāviśam
prekṣataś caiva [14]) me devas tatraivāntaradhīyata.

---

[12]) i.e., tvayā.
[13]) adverb.
[14]) gen. abs., § 114 VI.

X

Mbh. 12, 9, 4 ff. (12, 246 ff.)

Yudhiṣṭhira uvāca:

hitvā grāmyasukhācāraṃ tapyamāno mahat tapaḥ
araṇye phalamūlāśī cariṣyāmi mṛgaiḥ saha.
juhvāno 'gniṃ yathākālam ubhau kālāv upaspṛśan
kṛśaḥ parimitāhāraś carmacīrajaṭādharaḥ
śītavātātapasahaḥ kṣutpipāsāśramakṣamaḥ
tapasā vidhidṛṣṭena śarīram upaśoṣayan
manaḥkarṇasukhā nityaṃ śṛṇvann uccāvacā giraḥ
muditānām araṇyeṣu vasatāṃ mṛgapakṣiṇām
ājighran peśalān gandhān phullānāṃ vṛkṣavīrudhām
nānārūpān vane paśyan ramaṇīyān vanaukasaḥ,
ekāntaśīlo vimṛśan pakvāpakvena vartayan
pitṝn devāṃś ca vanyena vāgbhir adbhiś ca tarpayan.
evam āraṇyaśāstrāṇām ugram ugrataraṃ vidhim
sevamānaḥ pratīkṣiṣye dehasyāsya samāpanam.
athavaiko 'ham ekāham ekaikasmin vanaspatau
caran bhaikṣaṃ munir muṇḍaḥ kṣapayiṣye kalevaram
pāṃsubhiḥ samabhicchannaḥ śūnyāgārapratiśrayaḥ
vṛkṣamūlaniketo vā tyaktasarvapriyāpriyaḥ.

XI

Rāmāyaṇa 3, 11, 55 ff.

Ihaikadā kila krūro Vātāpir api celvalaḥ [1])
bhrātarau sahitāv āstāṃ brāhmaṇaghnau mahāsurau.
dhārayan brāhmaṇaṃ rūpam Ilvalaḥ saṃskṛtaṃ vadan [2])
āmantrayati viprān sa śrāddham uddiśya [3]) nirghṛṇaḥ.
bhrātaraṃ saṃskṛtaṃ kṛtvā tatas taṃ meṣarūpiṇam
tān dvijān bhojayāmāsa śrāddhadṛṣṭena [4]) karmaṇā.
tato bhuktavatāṃ teṣāṃ viprāṇām Ilvalo 'bravīt:
Vātāpe niṣkramasveti svareṇa mahatā vadan.
tato bhrātur vacaḥ śrutvā Vātāpir meṣavan nadan
bhittvā bhittvā [5]) śarīrāṇi brāhmaṇānāṃ viniṣpatat [6]).
brāhmaṇānāṃ sahasrāṇi tair evaṃ kāmarūpibhiḥ
vināśitāni saṃhatya nityaśaḥ piśitāśanaiḥ.
Agastyena [7]) tadā devaiḥ prārthitena [8]) maharṣiṇā
anubhūya kila śrāddhe [9]) bhakṣitaḥ sa mahāsuraḥ [10]).
tataḥ saṃpannam ity uktvā dattvā haste 'vanejanam
bhrātaraṃ niṣkramasveti Ilvalaḥ samabhāṣata.
sa tadā bhāṣamāṇaṃ tu bhrātaraṃ vipraghātinam
abravīt prahasan dhīmān Agastyo munisattamaḥ:

---

[1]) i.e., ca Ilvalaḥ.

[2]) like Brahmans speaking the correct standard speech.

[3]) § 117.

[4]) which one considers as a funeral gift and the funeral feast connected with it.

[5]) The duplication expresses the repetition.

[6]) § 57 V.

[7]) a ṛṣi.

[8]) i.e., prārthitāsuradvayasaṃhāreṇa "whom one asked for the destruction of the two Asuras".

[9]) after he had celebrated and enjoyed the śrāddha.

[10]) i.e., Vātāpi.

kuto niṣkramituṃ śaktir mayā jīrṇasya rakṣasaḥ
bhrātus tu meṣarūpasya gatasya Yamasādanam.
atha tasya vacaḥ śrutvā bhrātur nidhanasaṃśritam
pradharṣayitum ārebhe muniṃ krodhān niśācaraḥ.
so 'bhyadravad dvijendraṃ taṃ, muninā dīptatejasā
cakṣuṣānalakalpena nirdagdho nidhanaṃ gataḥ.

XII

Rām. 1, 45, 15 ff.

Pūrvaṃ kṛtayuge Rāma [1]) Diteḥ [2]) putrā mahābalāḥ
Aditeś [2]) ca mahābhāgā vīryavantaḥ sudhārmikāḥ [3]).
tatas teṣāṃ naravyāghra [4]) buddhir āsīn mahātmanām
amarā vijarāś caiva kathaṃ syāmo nirāmayāḥ?
teṣāṃ cintayatāṃ tatra buddhir āsīd vipaścitām
kṣīrodamathanaṃ kṛtvā rasaṃ prāpsyāma tatra vai.
tato niścitya mathanaṃ yoktraṃ kṛtvā ca Vāsukim [5])
manthānaṃ Mandaraṃ [6]) kṛtvā mamanthur amitaujasaḥ.
atha varṣasahasreṇa yoktrasarpaśirāṃsi ca
vamanto [7]) 'tiviṣaṃ [8]) tatra dadaṃśur daśanaiḥ śilāḥ.
utpapātāgnisaṃkāśaṃ [9]) hālāhalamahāviṣam.
tena dagdhaṃ jagat sarvaṃ sadevāsuramānuṣam.

[1]) This episode is told to the leading character of the Rāmāyaṇa, Rāma.

[2]) Diti and Aditi were two sisters, A. the mother of the gods, D. the mother of the enemies of the gods, i.e., the Daityas belonging to the Asuras.

[3]) i.e., āsan.

[4]) i.e., Rāma.

[5]) prince of serpents.

[6]) name of a sacred mountain.

[7]) the neutr. pl. is expected.

[8]) unusually effective poison.

[9]) i.e., śilādaśanāt.

atha devā mahādevaṃ Śaṅkaraṃ [10]) śaraṇārthinaḥ
jagmuḥ Paśupatiṃ Rudraṃ trāhi trāhīti tuṣṭuvuḥ.
evam uktas tato devair devadeveśvaraḥ prabhuḥ.
prādur āsīt tato 'traiva śaṅkhacakradharo Hariḥ.
uvācainaṃ smitaṃ kṛtvā Rudraṃ śūladharaṃ Hariḥ:
daivatair mathyamāne tu yat pūrvaṃ samupasthitam
tat tvadīyaṃ suraśreṣṭha, surāṇām agrato hi yat.
agrapūjām iha sthitvā gṛhāṇedaṃ viṣaṃ prabho.
ity uktvā ca suraśreṣṭhas [11]) tatraivāntaradhīyata.
devatānāṃ bhayaṃ dṛṣṭvā śrutvā vākyaṃ tu Śārṅgiṇaḥ
hālāhalaṃ viṣaṃ ghoraṃ saṃjagrāhāmṛtopamam [12]).
devān visṛjya deveśo jagāma bhagavān Haraḥ.
tato devāsurāḥ sarve mamanthū [13]) Raghunandana.
praviveśātha pātālaṃ manthānaḥ parvatottamaḥ [14]).
tato devāḥ sagandharvās tuṣṭuvur Madhusūdanam [15]):
tvaṃ gatiḥ sarvabhūtānāṃ viśeṣeṇa divaukasām.
pālayāsmān mahābāho, girim uddhartum arhasi.
iti śrutvā Hṛṣīkeśaḥ kāmaṭhaṃ rūpam āsthitaḥ
parvataṃ pṛṣṭhataḥ kṛtvā śiśye [16]) tatrodadhau Hariḥ.
parvatāgraṃ tu lokātmā hastenākramya Keśavaḥ [15])
devānāṃ madhyataḥ sthitvā mamantha Puruṣottamaḥ [15]).
atha varṣasahasreṇa āyurvedamayaḥ pumān
udatiṣṭhat sudharmātmā sadaṇḍaḥ sakamaṇḍaluḥ.
atha Dhanvantarir [17]) nāma, apsarāś ca suvarcasaḥ;

---

[10]) § 114 II.
[11]) Viṣṇu.
[12]) amṛtopamaṃ yathā bhavati tathā saṃjagrāha.
[13]) § 16.
[14]) Mandaraḥ.
[15]) Viṣṇu.
[16]) perf. of śī- "lie there".
[17]) i.e., udatiṣṭhat.

apsu nirmathanād eva rasāt tasmād varastriyaḥ
utpetur manujaśreṣṭha, tasmād apsaraso 'bhavan.
ṣaṣṭiḥ koṭyo 'bhavaṃs tāsām apsarāṇāṃ suvarcasām,
asaṃkhyeyās tu Kākutstha yās tāsāṃ paricārikāḥ.
Uccaiḥśravā hayaśreṣṭho maṇiratnaṃ ca Kaustubham
udatiṣṭhan naraśreṣṭha tathaivāmṛtam uttamam.
atha tasya kṛte Rāma mahān āsīt kulakṣayaḥ,
Adites tu tataḥ putrā Ditiputrān ayodhayan.
ekatām agaman sarve asurā rākṣasaiḥ saha,
yuddham āsīn mahāghoraṃ vīra trailokyamohanam.
yadā kṣayaṃ gataṃ sarvaṃ, tadā Viṣṇur mahābalaḥ
amṛtaṃ so 'harat tūrṇaṃ māyām āsthāya mohinīm.
ye gatā 'bhimukhaṃ Viṣṇum akṣaraṃ puruṣottamam
saṃpiṣṭās te tadā yuddhe Viṣṇunā prabhaviṣṇunā.
Aditer ātmajā vīrā Diteḥ putrān nijaghnire
asmin ghore mahāyuddhe Daiteyādityayor bhṛśam.
nihatya Ditiputrāṃs tu rājyaṃ prāpya Puraṃdaraḥ
śaśāsa mudito lokān sarṣisaṅghān sacāraṇān.

XIII

Rām. 2, 27 [1]

Evam uktā tu Vaidehī priyārhā priyavādinī
praṇayād eva saṃkruddhā bhartāram idam abravīt:
kim idaṃ bhāṣase Rāma vākyaṃ laghutayā dhruvam,
tvayā [2] yad apahāsyaṃ me śrutvā naravarottama.
vīrāṇāṃ rājaputrāṇāṃ śastrāstraviduṣāṃ nṛpa
anarham [3] ayaśasyaṃ ca na śrotavyaṃ tvayeritam.

---

[1] Rāma, who goes into exile, has exhorted his wife Sītā to remain at the court of his father. She answers him that she wants to follow him into the forest.

[2] tvayā yad uktaṃ tac chrutvāpahāsyaṃ me.

[3] + gen.

āryaputra pitā mātā bhrātā putras tathā snuṣā
svāni puṇyāni [4]) bhuñjānāḥ svaṃ svaṃ bhāgyam upāsate.
bhartur bhāgyaṃ tu nāry ekā prāpnoti puruṣarṣabha
ataś caivāham ādiṣṭā vane vastavyam ity api.
na pitā nātmajo nātmā na mātā na sakhījanaḥ
iha pretya ca nārīṇāṃ patir eko gatiḥ sadā.
yadi tvaṃ prasthito durgaṃ vanaṃ adyaiva Rāghava
agratas te gamiṣyāmi mṛdnantī kuśakaṇṭakān.
naya māṃ vīra viśrabdhaḥ, pāpaṃ mayi na vidyate.
prāsādāgre vimānair vā vaihāyasagatena vā
sarvāvasthāgatā bhartuḥ pādacchāyā viśiṣyate.
ahaṃ durgaṃ gamiṣyāmi vanaṃ puruṣavarjitam
nānāmṛgagaṇākīrṇaṃ śārdūlagaṇasevitam.
sukhaṃ vane nivatsyāmi [5]) yathaiva bhavane pituḥ
śuśrūṣamāṇā te nityaṃ niyatā brahmacāriṇī.
saha raṃsye tvayā vīra vaneṣu madhugandhiṣu,
tvaṃ hi kartuṃ vane śakto Rāma saṃparipālanam.
sāhaṃ [6]) tvayā gamiṣyāmi vanam adya na saṃśayaḥ [7]),
na te duḥkhaṃ kariṣyāmi nivasantī tvayā sadā.
agratas te gamiṣyāmi, bhokṣye bhuktavati tvayi;
icchāmi parataḥ śailān palvalāni sarāṃsi ca
draṣṭuṃ sarvatra nirbhītā tvayā nāthena dhīmatā.
saha tvayā viśālākṣa raṃsye paramanandinī
evaṃ varṣasahasrāṇi śataṃ vāpi tvayā saha.

---

[4]) = karmaphalāni.

[5]) § 72.

[6]) The sa which continues the discourse often has the significance of a conjunction; with aham, tvam, etc. it is frequently conclusive.

[7]) n. s. "without doubt", without grammatical connection with the sentence.

GLOSSARY

a°, before vowels *an*°, un- (negative).
akutobhaya-, a., not being afraid, not fearing.
akṣayya-, a., inexhaustible.
akṣara-, a., immortal, imperishable.
agni-, s. m., fire.
agra-, s. n., point, surface area; beginning; first born.
agratas, before, ahead of.
agrapūjā-, s. f. donation.
aṅga-, s. n., member, part, body.
ajā-, s. f. goat.
aṭ-, I, wander about.
aṇu-, a., very small.
aṇḍa-, s. n., egg.
atas, then, for this reason.
ati°, extremely, highly.
atigarīyas-, s. *ati* and *guru*-.
atithi-, s. m., guest.
ativāha-, s. n. excessive suffering or bearing.
ativiṣa-, a., extremely poisonous.
atiśaya-, s. m., excess.
atīva, extremely, exceedingly, very.
atyartha-, a., excessive, extreme.
atra, here, then.
atrāntare, meanwhile.
atraiva, s. *atra* and *eva*.
atha, thereupon, then, furthermore, thus, yet; *atha vā*, or.
atho, = *atha* + *u*.
ad-, II, eat.
adūra-, a., not far; s., nearness.
adṛṣṭa-, a., invisible; s., poisonous animal eluding the eye, vermin, . . . danger.
adbhuta-, a., amazing; s. n., marvel.
adya, today, now.
adri-, s. m., mountain, hill.
adhama-, a., low.
adhastāt, below.
adhipa-, s. m., lord.
adhobhāga-, s. m., the lower or inferior part.
anantara-, a., the nearest; adv., immediately afterwards.
anapakārin-, a., not doing harm.
anarha-, a., unworthy.
anala-, s. m., fire.
anāvṛṣṭi-, s. f., lack of rain.
anu, with gen., (immediately) afterwards; *tadanu*, hereupon.
anumantrita-, a., consecrated by a formula.
aneka-, a., several, many.
Antaka-, name of the god of death.
antarhita-, a. (p.p.p. of °*dhā*-), disappeared.
andha-, a., blind.
andhakāra-, s. m. darkness.
anna-, s. n. food.
anyatas, elsewhere.
anyathā, otherwise.
anyādṛś-, looking otherwise.
anvita-, a. (verb. adj. of *i*-), provided with.
ap-, s. f. pl. § 45 V, water.

apara-, a., the posterior, following, a different person, foreigner; *aparam*, further, besides.
aparādha-, s. m., mistake; offense.
apavāda-, s. m. rumor.
apahāsya-, a., to be laughed at.
apāhāya (*hā-*), with disregard, exception of.
api, also, even; (after numerals) all.
aputra-, a., without son.
apekṣā-, s. f., consideration, respect.
apsaras-, *apsarā-*, s. f., air nymph.
abhāva-, s. m., absence.
abhidhāna-, s. n., title, naming, name.
abhimukham, turned towards.
abhyantara-, s. n., the interior.
amara-, a., immortal.
amaratva-, s.n., immortality.
amita-, a., immense, immeasurable.
amitra-, s. m., enemy.
amṛta-, s.n., the potion of immortality.
ambara-, s. n., clothing.
ambhas-, s. n., water.
ayam, dem. pron., § 49.
ayaśasya-, a., inglorious.
Ayodhyā-, s. f., name of a city.
araṇya-, s. n., forest, desert.
ari-, s. m., enemy.
arjita-, s. *ṛj-*.
artha-, s. m., objective; thing, possession; *arthe*, *-am*, for the purpose of, on account of, for, for the sake of (after gen.); *ko 'rthaḥ* + instr., what is the benefit of the . . ., a . . .
artha-, X *arthayati*, ask for; with *pra*, approach someone with a request; wish.
arthin-, a., desiring.
ardha-, a., half; s. m. n., half.
arh-, I, earn, 2. p. *arhasi* takes the place of a polite imper., § 115 V.
arha-, a., deserving, worthy, fit.
alpa-, a., small, little.
avanejana-, s. n., washing, ablution.
avara-, a., low, inferior, trifling.
avasthā-, s. f., condition, situation.
avi-, s., sheep.
avikala-, a., of which nothing is lacking.
avitatha-, a., true.
aśana-, s. n., food, meal.
aśman-, s. m., stone.
aśru-, s. n., tear
aśva-, s. m., horse.
as-, II, be.
asaṃkhyeya-, a., countless.
asakṛt, often.
asi-, s. m., sword.
asura-, s. m., demon.
asṛj-, s. n., blood.
asau, that.
astamana-, s. n., sunset.
astra-, s. n., missile, arrow.
asthi-, s. n., § 45 II, bone.
asmākam, § 47.
ahi-, s. m., snake, serpent.
aho, interj. (astonishment, joy, mourning).
ākāṅkṣā-, s. f., wish.
ākāra-, s. m., form, figure, configuration.
ākīrṇa-, a., covered, full; s. *ā-kṝ-*.

āgāra-, s. n., house.
ācāra-, s. m., (good) conduct.
ācārya-, s. m., teacher (esp. of the Veda).
ājñā-, s. f., command.
āḍhya-, a., rich.
ātapa-, s. m., heat of the sun.
ātura-, a., sick; °*ā*., sick on account of . . .
ātmaja-, s. m., son.
ātman-, s. m., self, breath, soul; also as refl. pron.
Āditya-, s. m., sons of Aditi, name of a class of gods.
ānata-, s. *nam-*.
āp-, V, obtain, reach, attain; with *ava*, *pra*, the same; with *saṃ-pra*, come, arrive at.
āpad-, s. f., misfortune.
āpanna-, a., fallen (into misfortune).
āmra-, s. m., mango tree.
āyudha-, s. n., weapon.
āyurvedamaya-, a., containing the science of medicine in itself.
āyus-, s. n., life.
āraṇya-, a., pertaining to the wilderness.
ārabdha-, s., *rabh-*.
ārta-, a., depressed, grieved.
ārya-, s. m., Aryan.
āryaputra-, honorable mode of address of the husband.
āśin-, a., eating.
āśrita- (*śri-* with *ā*), a., present at, having reached for something.
ās- II, mid. sit, remain in a state, etc.; with *upa*, apply oneself to a thing, take part in something.
āṣakta-, s. *sañj-*.
āsana-, s. n., seat.
āsanna-, s. n., vicinity, proximity.
āsīt, s. *as-* II.
āha, (he) spoke.
āhāra-, s. m., nourishment.

i-, II, go; with *adhi*, mid., study, learn; with *ava*, comprehend, become acquainted with; with *ā*, come; with *abhi-ā*, come near; with *pari-ā*, return; with *ud*, rise; with *upa*, approach; with *pra*, die.
icchati, s. I *iṣ-*.
itara-, a., other.
itarathā, in another way, otherwise.
iti, § 119.
°*indra-*, s. m., the first, chief.
indriya-, s. n., sense.
iva, as, just as; as if.
I *iṣ-*, *icchati* (§ 61) wish; with *anu*, seek.
II *iṣ-*, with *pra*, X, send.
iṣu-, s. m. f., arrow.
iṣudhi-, s. m. f., quiver.
iṣṭa- (verb. adj. of I *iṣ-*), desired, dear.
iha, here.
īkṣ-, *īkṣate*, with *ava*, look at, perceive; keep in view; with *pra*, catch sight of; with *prati*, wait for, await; with *vi*, catch sight of, recognize.
īdṛśa-, a., such.
īps- I, wish.
īrita- (p.p.p. *īr-* X), uttered, pronounced.
īrṣyā-, s. f., jealousy.
īśa-, s. m., lord.
īśvara-, s. m., lord.

u, slightly emphat. part.
ukta-, a., said.
ugra- a., mighty.
uccaya-, s. m., quantity, s. *śiloccaya-*.
uccāvaca-, a., multifarious, various.
ucchrita-, a., high.
uttama-, superl., highest, most excellent.
utsaṅga-, s. n., lap, haunch.
utsādana-, s. n., annihilating.
udaka-, s. n., water.
udadhi-, s. m., sea.
uddiśya (ger., *diś-*), on account of, for, according to; cf. § 117.
udvāha-, s. m., wedding.
upakṣaya-, s.m., disappearance, exhaustion, expense.
upadeśa-, s. m., instruction.
upadrava-, s. m. misfortune.
°*upama-*, a., similar.
upari, prep., with abl., after, according to.
upalipta-, a., smeared, anointed.
upāya-, s. m., means, remedy.
upeta-, a. (p.p.p. *upa-i-*), with instr., provided with.
ubha-, both.
Umā, the wife of Śiva.
urvarita-, a., left over.
urvī-, s. f., earth.
uvāca, s. *vac-*.
uṣita-, a., s. *vas-*, dwell.
ūrdhva-, a., upright.

ṛj-, I and *arjayati*, obtain.
ṛte, without, except (with abl.).
ṛṣabha-, s. m., bull.
ṛṣi-, s. m., wise man, holy man.

eka-, one, alone; also indef. article.
ekatā-, s. f., union.
ekadā, one day.
ekadṛṣṭi-, s. f., a glance directed at an object.
ekadeśa-, s. m., a place.
ekarātra-, s. n., the duration of a night.
ekānta-, s. m., solitary place.
ekāham, for an entire day.
ekaika-, a., each one.
etat, § 48.
etāvat-, (only) so much, such.
eva, just, already, quite, only.
evaṃvidha-, a., such.
evam, so, thus.

ojas-, s. n., strength, power.

kaccid, interrogative part.; ± perhaps.
kacchapa-, s. m., tortoise.
kaṭa-, s. m., mat.
kaṇṭaka-, s. m., thorn.
kaṇṭha-, s. m., neck, throat.
katham, how?; *katham api*, with effort; *na k. cana*, in no way whatsoever.
kathā-, s.f., narration, conversation.
kadā, when?; *kadācid*, once upon a time, at some time or other; *na kadācid*, never
kanyā-, s. f., maiden, girl.
kamaṇḍalu-, s. m. n., water-jar.
kamp-, I mid., tremble; caus., cause to tremble.
kambala-, s. m. n., a woolen garment, gown.
kara-, s. m., hand, ray.

karaṇa-, s. n., the doing, the action.
karapatra-, s. n., saw.
karṇa-, s. m., ear; *ākarṇayati*, hear.
kardama-, s. m., dirt.
karman-, s. n., deed, action, work, business.
kal-, with *ā*, *ākalayati*, grasp, possess.
kalaha-, s. m., strife, contention.
kalevara-, s. m. n., body.
kalpa-, s. m., manner and way.
kavi-, s. m., poet.
Kākutstha-, Rāma.
kāma-, s. m., love; object of desire; *kāmam*, adv., gladly, certainly.
kāmaṭha-, a., peculiar to a tortoise.
kāmarūpin-, a., assuming a form at will.
Kāmyaka-, name of a forest.
kāya-, s. m., body.
kāyastha-, s. m., writer, scribe.
kāraṇa-, s. n., cause.
kārya-, a., to be done; s. n., matter.
kāla-, s. m., time; also personif. of time, of death.
kālasarpa-, s. m., a certain poisonous snake.
Kāśī-, s. f., Benares.
kāṣṭha-, s. n., wood, piece of wood.
kiṃcid, § 50.
kim, how?, why?
kimartham, why?
kiyat-, a., small, slight.
kirāta-, s. m., member of a mountain tribe.
kila, certainly, namely.
kīrti-, s. f., fame.
kīlaka-, s. m., wedge, peg.
kuṭīraka-, s. m., cottage, hut.
kuṭṭanī-, s. f., procuress.
kutas, whence?
kutra, where? whither?
kutrāpi, somewhere, to some place.
kupita-, a., angry.
Kuru-, name of a people and of an ancestor.
Kurukṣetra-, s. n., name of a country.
kula-, s. n., race, family.
kuśa-, s. m., Kuśa grass.
kūṭa-, a., cunning, deceitful.
kṛ-, VIII, make, do, carry out, act, etc.; caus., cause to be done; *kiṃ kriyate* + instr., what should one do with . . .
kṛtaghna-, a., ungrateful.
kṛtayuga-, s. n., the first or "golden" age.
kṛte (*kṛ-*), on account of, for (+ gen.).
kṛtya-, a. (grdv of *kṛ-*), to be done; s. n., obligation, business.
kṛpā-, s. f., sympathy, compassion.
kṛśa-, a., lean, emaciated.
kṛṣ-, I, pull; with *ā*, draw on, tense, stretch; with *vi*, bend (a bow).
kṝ-, VI *kirati*, scatter; with *ā*, strew; with *ava*, strew, spill; with *sam-ava*, flood.
kairāta-, a., concerning the Kirāta- (a despised mountain tribe).

koṭi-, s. f., utmost point, bent end; ten million.
kopa-, s. m., anger.
kolāhala-, s. m., shouting.
kautuka-, s. n., curiosity, what arouses curiosity, festivity, solemn ceremony.
kaulika-, s. m., weaver.
kram-, I (§ 61 II), step; with *ā*, approach, come near, ascend, step into something, come into force, begin; with *nis*, go out.
krī-, IX, buy.
krīḍ-, I, *krīḍati*, play.
krīḍana-, s. n., play, game.
krudh-, IV, be angry.
kruddha-, a., angry.
krūra-, a., cruel.
krodha-, s. m., anger.
klānta-, a., tired.
kva, where?, whither?
kṣama-, a., bearing, suited for something.
kṣaya-, s. m., decline, destruction.
kṣal-, with *pra*, *prakṣālayati*, wash.
kṣāma-, a., dried up, dessicated.
kṣi-, X, destroy, annihilate.
kṣip-, VI, throw; with *pra*, throw into.
kṣipra-, a., quick.
kṣīra-, s. m. n., milk.
kṣīroda-, s. m., sea of milk.
kṣudh-, s. f., *kṣudhā-*, s. f. hunger.
kṣubhita-, a., in excitement.
kṣura-, s. m., razor.
kṣetra-, s. n., field.
khaṭvā-, s. f., bedstead.
khaḍga-, s. m., sword.
khaṇḍa-, s. m. n., gap, lacuna, piece; *khaṇḍaśas*, into pieces.
khāta-, a., dug up, rooted up.
khād-, I, eat, devour.
khura-, s. m., hoof.
khyāta-, a., famous.

Gaṅgā-, s. f., Ganges.
gaja-, s. m., elephant.
gaṇa-, s. m., troop, crowd.
gata- (verb. adj. of *gam-*), gone; s. n., going, walk, pace.
gati-, s. f., path, way, way out, refuge, condition.
gad-, *gadati*, speak, say.
gantavya- grdv. (§ 116 VII), (one) should go.
gandha-, s. m., smell, odor.
gandharva-, name of a class of mythol. beings.
gandhin-, a., having a smell.
gam-, I *gacchati*, go, go away, pass (time). With *adhi*, find out; with *anu*, follow; with *ava*, recognize; with *ā*, come; with *upa-ā*, approach, come near; with *sam-ā*, come together, coalesce; with *nis*, set out; with *prati*, return.
gariṣṭha-, sup. of *guru-*.
gardabha-, s. m., ass.
gardabhī-, s. f., she-ass.
garbhin-, a., f. *-ī*, pregnant.
garva-, s. m., conceit.
gā-, go.
gā(y)-, I, *gāyati*, sing.
gir-, s. f., voice.
giri-, s. m., mountain, hill.
gīta-, s. n., song.
guṇa-, s. m., virtue.
guṇavat-, a., excellent.
guṇṭh- with *ava*, cover, coat.
guru-, a., heavy, hard, vener-

able; s. authority, person of respect, teacher, father.
Gurjara-, name of a country.
gṛha-, s. n., house.
gṛhastha-, s. m., the married Brahman in charge of his own household; also adj.
gṛhīta-, p.p.p. of *grah-*.
gṛhītvā, ger. of *grah-*.
go-, s. (§ 31), ox, cow.
gocara-, s. m., domain, range.
govṛṣa-, s. m., bull.
grabh-, = *grah-*.
grah-, IX, take, buy; with *prati*, accept; with *sam*, seize.
grāma-, s. m., village.
grāmya-, pertaining to the village.
ghaṭ-, *ghaṭati*, get into; with *ud*, X, open.
ghaṭa-, s. m., pot.
ghaṇṭā-, s. f., bell.
ghāta-, s. m., blow, homicide.
ghātaka-, a., destroying.
ghātin-, a., killing.
ghora-, a., terrible.
°*ghna-*, a., killing.
ghrā-, I *jighrati*, smell; with *ā*, smell.

ca, and.
cakra-, s. n., wheel, circle, discus.
cakṣus-, s. n., eye.
cañcalatā-, s. f., mobility, moodiness.
caṭaka-, s. m., sparrow.
catur-, § 54, four.
caturtha-, a., fourth.
catvāras, § 54, four.
candra-, s. m., moon.
car-, I, go; with *pra-ud*, caus., cause to sound.
caraṇa-, s. m. n., foot.
carman-, s. n., skin, hide.
cal-, *calati*, move, go.
calana-, s. n., movement, creeping, crawling.
cāra-, s. m., scout.
cāraṇa-, s. m., heavenly singer.
ci-, with *nis*, determine, decide.
citā-, s. f., funeral pile, pyre.
citta-, s. n., mind.
cint-, X, think, consider; with *sam*, reflect, consider.
cintā-, s. f., thought, idea, worry.
cira-, long (of time); *na cireṇa*, after not a long time.
cirāt, after a long time, finally.
cīra-, s. n., a thin and long piece of bark.
cīvara-, s.n., dress of rags.
cūḍāmaṇi-, s. m., jewel.
cūrṇita-, a., shattered.
ced, if.
cora-, s. m., thief.
caura-, s. m., thief.
chad-, *chādayati*, cover; with *sam-abhi* and *pra*, cover.
chāyā-, s. f., shadow, shade.
chid-, VII, split, cut off.
chidra-, s. n., hole.
cheda-, s. m., cutting off.

°*ja-*, arisen from . . .
jagat-, s. n., world.
jaṅghā-, s. f., leg.
jaṭā-, s. f., plait.
jaṭhara-, s. n., belly.
jan-, *jāyate*, be born, arise, become; with *sam*, be born, arise, become.
jana-, s. m., human being, pl. people.

janapada-, s. m., people, land.
jananī-, s. f., mother.
Janamejaya-, name of a king.
jantu-, s. m., creature.
jap-, I, mutter to oneself.
jambāla-, s. m., mud.
jala-, s. n., water.
jalāśaya-, s. m., pond.
jalaukas-, s. f., leech.
jāta-, p.p.p. of *jan-*.
jātīya-, a., belonging to the class . . ., family . . .
jānāmi, s. *jñā-*.
jānu-, s. n., knee.
jāmātṛ-, s. m., son-in-law.
jāyā-, s. f., wife.
ji-, I, defeat, conquer.
jighrat-, s. *ghrā-*.
jita-, (p.p.p. of *ji-*), defeated, conquered.
jīrṇa-, a., old, dilapidated.
jīv-, *jīvati*, live, caus. *jīvāpayati*, make living, animate, vivify.
jīva-, s. n., life.
jīvita-, a., revived; s. n., life.
°*jña-*, a., knowing, acquainted with.
jñā-, IX, *jānāti*, know; with *anu*, dismiss; with *sam* + *ā*, learn; with *pari*, recognize, know exactly; with *vi*, caus., cause someone to know.
jñāna-, s. n., knowledge, insight.
jvalita-, a., blazing.

tatas, from there, there, thereupon, then.
tatra, there, therein; + *eva*, ibid., just there, at the very same place.
tathā, so, likewise, and; *tathā* + *api* (*eva*), nevertheless.
tathya-, a., true; s. n., truth.
tad, adv., there; at that time; therefore.
tadanantaram, s. *anantara-*.
tadanu, s. *anu*.
tadā, then, thereupon.
tadānīm, at that time.
tanu-, s. f., body.
tanu-, a., thin, fine.
tap-, I, be warm, heat up.
tapas tap-, practice asceticism.
tapas-, s. n., heat; asceticism; *tapasyati*, practice asceticism.
tapasvin-, a., ascetic; s. m., ascetic.
tamāla-, s. m., name of a tree.
taru-, s. m., tree.
tarhi, then, therefore.
tala-, s. m. n., surface; palm of the hand.
taskara-, s. m., robber.
tasmād (abl. s. n.) therefore.
tāḍ-, X, strike.
tāpasa-, s. m., ascetic.
tāvat, a., so much; adv. so long, first, meanwhile, immediately.
tīra-, s. n., bank, shore.
tu, but.
tulā-, s. f., balance.
tuṣ-, IV, be pleased, caus., satisfy; with *pari*, caus., satisfy completely.
tuṣṭa-, a., satisfied, content.
tūrṇam, adv., quickly.
tūṣṇīm, adv., silently.
tṛṇa-, s. n., grass, straw.
tṛtīya-, a., third.
tṛp-, IV, be satisfied; X, satisfy, satiate, please, appease.

tṛ-, I and VI, inf. *tar(i)tum*, cross over, overcome.
tejas-, s. n., sharpness, fervor, passion, power, energy, moral and magic power.
tyaj-, I, leave, abandon, desert; *pari*, leave, give up.
tyāga-, s. m., liberality.
trayaḥ, § 54, three.
tras-, I, tremble; caus., frighten.
trā-, II, protect.
trāṇa-, s. n., protection.
tridaśa-, the 33 gods.
trailokya-, s. n., the three worlds.
Tryambaka-, = Śiva.
tvadīya-, a., your, yours.
tvam, § 47, you (fam. and polite).
tvādṛśa-, a., one such as you, one like you.

daṃpati-, du. *-tī-*, married couple.
daṃś-, I (§ 61 III), *daśati*, bite.
daṃṣṭrā-, s. f., pointed tooth, fang.
dakṣa-, a., able.
dagdha-, p.p.p. s. *dah-*.
daṇḍa-, s. m. n., stick, staff, power, punishment.
datta-, p.p.p. of *dā-*, given.
danta-, s. m., tooth.
Damayantī, name of a queen.
darpa-, s. m., insolence.
daśana-, s. m., tooth.
daṣṭa- (verb. adj. of *daṃś-*), bitten.
dasyu-, s. m., an evil or hostile man.
dah-, I, burn, consume by fire; with *nis* and *vi-nis*, burn.
dahyat-, a. (part.), burning.
dā-, III, give; with *ā*, take, *ā-dā-vacanam*, begin to speak; with *pra*, lend, give; give in marriage.
dāna-, s. n., liberality.
dānavat-, a., generous.
dāyaka-, a., giving.
dāridrya-, s. n., poverty.
dāru-, s. n., wood.
dāruṇa-, a., terrible, rough.
dāva-, s. m., forest fire.
dāsa-, s. m., servant.
dāsī-, s. f., slave girl.
dina-, s. m., day.
divasa-, s. m., day.
divākara-, s. m., sun.
divaukas-, s. m., inhabitant of heaven.
divya-, a., heavenly, divine.
diś-, s. f., region of the heavens.
diś-, VI, show, point out, etc.; with *ā*, *prati-ā* and *sam-ā*, order.
dīna-, a., sad.
dīp-, *dīpyate*, blaze; int. blaze strongly, illuminate brightly.
dīpta-, a., blazing, radiant.
dīrghasattra-, s. n., a protracted Soma celebration.
duḥkha-, a., unpleasant; s. n., misfortune, suffering.
duḥkhita-, a., concerned.
duḥsparśa-, a., hard to touch.
dundubhi-, s. m., drum, kettle-drum.
durga-, a., impassable.
durgati-, s. f., misery.
Durgā-, s. f., name of a goddess.
durjana-, s. m., a bad man.
durbala-, a., weak.
durbhikṣa-, s. n., famine.
durlabha-, a., hard to attain.

duh-, II, milk.
duhitṛ-, s. f., daughter.
dūra-, a., far; s. n., distance.
dṛ-, IX, burst; *vi-dārayati*, burst, split.
dṛḍha-, a., firm, strong, violent.
dṛś-, see.
dṛṣṭa- (verb. adj. of *dṛś-*), seen; established.
dṛṣṭi-, s. f., perceiving.
deya-, grdv. of *dā-*.
deva-, s. m., god; voc. *deva*, also sire.
devana-, s. n., game of dice.
devī-, s. f., goddess.
deśa-, s. m., place, spot, region, land.
deśāntara-, s., foreign country.
deha-, s. m. n., body.
daiva-, s. n., fate.
daivata-, s. n., divinity.
dogdhrī-, giving milk.
doṣa-, s. m., mistake, guilt, sin.
drava-, a., fluid.
dravya-, s. n., property, wealth.
dru-, I, run, melt; with *abhi*, hasten towards, approach vigorously, set to with a will.
druma-, s. m., tree.
drohin-, a., betraying.
dvaya-, s. n., pair.
dvija-, s. m., Brahman.
dvitīya-, a., second.
dviṣ-, II, hate.
dviṣ-, s. m., enemy.
dvīpin-, s. m., panther.
dhana-, s. n., possession, wealth, money.
Dhanañjaya-, = Arjuna.
dhanin-, a., rich (esp. in land), opulent.
dhanus-, s. n., bow.
dhanuṣmat-, a., provided with a bow.
dhanya-, a., fortunate.
Dhanvantari-, the doctor of the gods.
dham-, I, blow; with *vi-*, cause to disperse.
dhara-, a., bearing.
dharma-, s. m., law, precept, duty, etc.
dharmavat-, a., just.
dhā-, III, put, place; (+ dat.) direct toward; with *antar*, pass.,disappear; with *abhi*, address; with *ava*, mid., pay attention; with *ni*, place, set down, place, place into; with *vi*, make, fabricate.
dhātrī-, s. f., wet nurse.
dhārmika-, a., virtuous.
dhāv-, *dhāvati*, run; with *abhi*, run straight at or toward a thing.
dhīmat-, a., intelligent, wise.
dhīra-, a., resolute; wise.
dhūma-, s. m., smoke.
dhūsara-, a., gray.
dhṛ-, X, *dhārayati*, bear, hold; obtain, possess; with *ava-*, X, get acquainted with; with *vi*, detain, arrest.
°*dhṛk-*, bearing.
dhṛṣ-, with *pra*, X, offend someone, overcome.
dhenu-, s. f., cow.
dhairya-, s. n., steadfastness, firmness.
dhyāna-, s. n., meditation.
dhruva-, a., fixed, constant.
dhvaja-, s. m., flag.

na, not.
nagara-, s. n., town, city.
nagarī-, s. f., town, city.
nad-, I, cry, sound, roar, bellow.
nadī-, s. f., river.
nandana-, s. m., son.
nandin-, a., having joy in.
nam-, I, humble oneself; with *ā*, stoop, bow; with *pra*, bow before.
nara-, s. m., man.
naraka-, s. m., hell.
naś-, IV, get lost, perish; with *vi*, get lost, perish; caus., destroy.
nāga-, s. m., elephant, snake, serpent.
nātha-, s. m., protector, ruler.
nānā°, various, manifold.
nāman-, s. n., name; acc. s. *nāma*, by name; namely.
nārī-, s. f., woman, wife.
nāśana-, s. n., destroying, annihilation.
nikartana-, s.n., massacre, slaughter.
niketa-, s. m., dwelling.
nija-, a., own, native or inherent to.
nityam, always.
nityaśaḥ, always.
nidrā-, s. f., sleep.
nidhana-, s. m. n., death.
nibhṛta-, a., hidden, concealed.
niyata-, s. *yam-*.
nirāmaya-, a., healthy, sound.
nirāśībhūta-, a., who has given up hope.
nirāhāra-, a., refraining from food.
nirghṛṇa-, a., cruel, inhuman, bloodthirsty.
nirdagdha-, s. *dah-*.
nirdhana-, a., poor.
nirbhīta-, a., fearless.
nirmathana-, s. n., churning.
nilaya-, s. m., nest.
niśācara-, s. m., (nocturnal) monster.
niśita-, a., sharp.
niśītha-, s. m., night.
niśceṣṭa-, a., motionless.
nisarga-, s. m., nature.
nī-, I, lead, take along; with *ā*, bring; with *sam-ā*, bring together, bring up (to the speaker), bring home; with *pari*, marry.
nīca-, a., low, common.
nīḍa-, s. n., nest.
nūnam, certainly.
nṛ-, s. m., man, human being.
nṛpa-, s. m., prince.
nṛpati-, s. m., prince.
no cet, if not —.
nau-, s. f., ship.

pakva-, s. n., food.
pakṣin-, s. m., bird.
pac-, I, cook.
pañcatva-, s. n., death.
pañcama-, a., fifth.
paṭh-, *paṭhati*, recite aloud.
paṇḍita-, a., intelligent, learned.
pat-, I, fall, fall into; p.p.p. *patita-*; with *ā*, unexpectedly fall to a person's lot; with *ut*, rise, arise; with *ni*, caus., cause to fall, cast or hurl down; with *vi*, caus., fell, slay; with *vinis*, come forth.
pati-, s. m., lord.
patnī-, s. f., lady, wife.

path-, s. m., § 45 III, path, road.
pad-, IV mid., fall away, go to; with *vi-ā*, caus., destroy; with *ut*, arise; with *nis* caus., prepare; with *pra*, come to, go to; with *sam*, fall to one's lot.
para-, a., further, later; foreign; best, highest; s. m., enemy; at the end of a comp., intent on.
paratas, further, abl. of *para-*.
parantapa-, a., tormenting the enemy.
param, thereupon; nevertheless.
parama-, a., highest, best; —°, extremely, very.
paraśu-, s. m., axe.
parārtha-, s. m., the advantage of others.
parigraha-, s. m., attainment, possession.
paricārikā-, s. f., servant girl or woman.
parijñāta-, a., recognized.
paripūrita-, s. I. *pṝ-*.
paripūrṇa- (s. I. *pṝ-*), entirely filled.
parimita-, a., limited, small.
parisamāpta- (*āp-*), a., completely ended.
paruṣa-, a., rough, uneven.
parvata-, s. m., mountain, hill.
palāy-, *palāyate*, flee.
palvala-, s. n., pond.
paś-, IV, see.
paśu-, s. m., cattle; also a single head.
Paśupati-, = Śiva.
paścāt, afterward, later.
pā-, I, *pibati*, drink.
pā-, II, protect.
pāṃsu-, s. m., dust, sand.
pāṇi-, s. m., hand.
pāṇḍitya-, s. n., learning, erudition.
pāṇḍuratā-, s. f., white color.
pāta-, s. m., fall.
pātāla-, s. n., nether world.
pāda-, s. m., foot.
pāpa-, s. n., evil, sin, harm.
Pārikṣita-, son of Parikṣit.
pārthiva-, s. m., prince.
pārśva-, s. m. n., side, vicinity.
pāla-, s. m., guard, keeper; *pālayati*, guard, save, rescue.
pāvaka-, s. m., fire.
pāśa-, s. m., noose, fetter.
pāśupata-, a., consecrated to Śiva-Paśupati, concerning Śiva-Paśupati.
pitṛ-, s. m., father.
pitṛpaitāmaha-, a., inherited.
pināka-, s. m. n., the club and bow of Śiva.
pipāsā-, s. f., thirst.
pipīlika-, s. m., ant.
pibati, s. *pā-*.
piśita-, s. n., flesh.
piṣ-, VII, with *sam*, crush.
pīḍ-, X, press, torture.
puṇya-, a., favorable, fortunate, fair, handsome.
putra-, s. m., son.
putrī-, s. f., daughter.
punar, again, back; in contrast.
pumaṃs-, s. m., § 45 IV, man.
pura-, s. n., town, city.
Puraṃdara-, = the god Indra.
purī-, s. f., stronghold, town.
puruṣa-, s. m., man.
puruṣottama-, s. m., the highest spirit, Viṣṇu.

puṣkara-, s. n., tip of the elephant's trunk.
puṣṭa-, a., well nourished.
pustaka-, s. n., book.
pū-, IX, purify, cleanse.
pūga-, s. m., quantity.
pūj-, X, honor.
pūjā-, s. f., honoring.
pūjya- (grdv. of *pūj-*), to be honored.
pūrita-, a., filled (p.p.p. of I. *pṝ-* X).
pūrṇa- (to I. *pṝ-*), full, filled, replete.
pūrva-, a., earlier; adv. formerly, earlier.
pūruṣa-, = *puruṣa-*.
pṛthivī-, s. f., earth.
pṛṣṭa-, p.p.p. of *prach-*.
pṛṣṭha-, s. n., back, posterior side; *pṛṣṭhatas*, from, toward the rear or back.
I *pṝ-*, IX, fill; with *pari*, caus. (p.p.p. *paripūrita-*) make full.
II *pṝ-*, *pārayati*, with acc., resist.
peśala-, a., agreeable, charming.
paitāmaha-, a., pertaining to a grandfather, grandfatherly.
potabhaṅga-, s. m., shipwreck.
pautra-, s. m., grandson.
paura-, s. m., citizen.
prakāra-, s. m., manner, way, kind.
prakopa-, s. m., anger.
pracalana-, s. n., creeping.
prach-, *pṛcchati*, § 61 I, ask.
prajā-, s. f. pl., subjects, vassals.
praṇaya-, s. m., familiarity, confidence; abl., frankly.
pratikṣaṇam, continually, each moment.
pratiśraya-, s. m., refuge; dwelling.
pratīkāra-, s. m., remedy, antidote.
prathama-, a., first.
pradeśa-, s. m., place, region.
pradhāna-, a., most excellent.
prapanna-, p.p.p. of *pad-* with *pra*.
prabhaviṣṇu-, a., mighty; s. m., lord.
prabhu-, s. m., lord.
prabhūta-, a., much, copious.
prayatna-, s. m., effort.
prayojana-, s. n., purpose, benefit.
pravivāda-, s. m., strife, quarrel.
prasanna-, a., merciful.
prasava-, s. m., procreation.
prasupta-, a., fallen asleep.
prastāva-, s. m., opportunity, occasion.
prahara-, s. m., a time lapse of about 3 hours.
prahāra-, s. m., blow.
prāñjali-, a., extending the hands (as sign of respect).
prāṇa-, s. m., breath of life.
prādur as-, appear.
prāpta-, s. *āp-*.
prārthita-, s. *arthayati* with *pra*.
prāvṛṣ-, s. f., rainy season.
prāsāda-, s. m., palace.
priya-, a., dear; *priyā-*, the beloved.
priyavāda-, s. m., friendly words.
priyavādin-, a., saying pleasant things.
prīta-, a., delighted, pleased.
prītimat-, a., delighted, content.
pretya, s. *i-*.
prerita-, s. *īr-*.

preṣyā-, s. f., servant.
proccārita-, a., p.p.p. s. *car-* with *pra-ud.*
protha-, s. m. n., snout.
plu-, I, swim.
phala-, s. n., fruit.
phulla-, a., blooming.

baddha- (p.p.p. of *bandh-*), bound.
bandh-, IX, bind.
bandhu-, s. m., relative, friend.
bala-, s. n., power, army.
balavat-, *balin-*, a., powerful.
bahiṣkṛ-, VIII, exclude.
bahu-, a., much.
bāṇa-, s. m., arrow.
bāndhava-, s. m., relative.
bāla-, s., child.
bālaka-, s., small child.
bāhu, s. m., arm.
buddhi-, s. f., understanding, intellect, mind, opinion.
buddhimat-, a., understanding.
budh-, I, awaken; recognize.
bṛhat-, a., great.
brahmacārin-, a., practicing chastity.
brahmavid-, s. m., one who knows piety or divine knowledge, wise man.
brāhmaṇa-, a., belonging to a Brahman; s. m., Brahman.
brāhmaṇī-, s. f., a Brahman woman.
brū-, II *bravīti*, speak.
bhakṣ- I and X, eat.
bhakṣita-, p.p.p. of *bhakṣ-*.
bhagavat-, a., noble, venerable.
bhagna-, s. *bhañj-*.
bhaṅga-, s. m., a breaking, fracture.
bhañj-, VII, verb. adj. *bhagna-*, break off, shatter.
bhan-, speak.
bhadra-, fortunate, favorable, good; voc. f. *bhadre* my good lady.
bhaya-, s. n., danger, fear.
bhayānaka-, a., terrible, sinister.
bhartṛ-, s. m., husband.
bhavat-, nom. *bhavān* with the 3rd pers. of the verb, polite pron. of the 2nd pers.
bhavana-, s. n., dwelling.
bhasman-, s. n., ash.
bhāga-, s. m., part.
bhāgya-, a., fortunate; s. n., luck, fortune.
bhāra-, s. m., burden.
bhāryā-, s. f., wife.
bhāṣ-, I, speak; with *sam*, speak; with *prati*, answer.
bhikṣā-, s. f., alms.
bhikṣu-, s. m., beggar, mendicant friar.
bhitti-, s. f., wall.
bhid-, VII, split, break.
bhiṣaj-, s. m., doctor.
bhukta-, a., eaten (lit. enjoyed); s. n., food.
bhuj-, VII mid., eat, enjoy.
bhujaṃgama-, s. m., snake.
bhū-, s. f., earth, ground.
bhū-, I., flourish, become, be; caus., promote, cause to develop, nurture; with *anu*, feel, enjoy, suffer; with *abhi*, be superior, overpower; with *pra*, prevail, be able.
bhūta-, s. n., being, sinister being.
bhūpati-, s. m., prince.
bhūpāla-, s. m., prince.

bhūmi-, s. f., earth, ground.
bhūyas, adv., more, very, besides, further.
bhūri-, a., much, significant.
bhūṣaṇa-, s. n., adornment, ornament, jewelry.
bhṛ- I and III, bear, carry.
Bhṛgutuṅga-, name of a sacred mountain.
bhṛt-, bearing, possessing, bringing.
bhṛtya-, s. m., servant.
bhṛśam, very.
bheṣaja-, s. n., remedy, antidote.
bhaikṣa-, s. n., begging; begged food.
bho(ḥ), O!
bhojana-, s. n., food, meal.
bhram-, *bhramati*, *bhrāmyati*, roam about; with *pari*, roam about.
bhrātṛ-, s. m., brother.

maṇi-, s. m., jewel.
mata-, verb. adj. of *man-*; s. n., opinion.
mati-, s. f., understanding, reason.
matimat-, a., intelligent.
matsya-, s. m., fish.
math-, I and IX, whirl.
mathana-, s. n., churning.
madīya-, a., my, mine.
madhu, s. n., honey; a., sweet.
Madhusūdana-, Viṣṇu.
madhya-, s. n., middle; a., in the middle; *madhyatas*, adv. in the middle.
madhyama-, a., middle, midmost.
madhyāhna-, s. m., noon.
manas-, s. n., mind, intellect, feeling.
Manu, father and lord of men.
manuja-, s. m., human being, man.
manuṣya-, s. m., human being, man.
manogata-, s. n., thought, desire, longing.
manoratha-, s. m., wish.
manohara-, a., charming.
mantra-, s. m., sacred text, formula, *mantrayati*, advise; with *ā*, X, invite.
mantravādin-, s. m., reciter of spells or incantations.
mantrin-, s. m., adviser, minister.
manthāna-, s. m., churn staff.
mandaṃ mandam, quite slowly.
Mandara-, s. m., name of a sacred mountain.
marut-, s. m., wind.
markaṭa-, s. m., ape.
martya-, s. m., mortal.
mardana-, a., torturing, crushing.
mahat-, a., great, large. fem. *mahatī*.
mahā-, at the beginning of comp., great.
mahātman-, a., noble, eminent, mighty.
mahābhāga-, a., very distinguished, prominent.
mahārāja-, a great king, prince, ruler.
mahāsattva-, a., noble; s. m., a noble creature.
mahiṣī-, s. f., female buffalo.
mahī-, s. f., earth.
mahendra-, s. m., great chief.
mā, not (prohibitive).
mā-, III, *mimīte*, measure; with *anu*, conclude.
māṃsa-, s. n., flesh.

mātula-, a., belonging to the mother's brother.
mātṛ-, s. f., mother.
māna-, s. m., honor; *mānayati*, honor.
mānasa-, s. n., mind, intellect.
mānuṣa-, s. m., human being, man.
māyā-, s. f., illusion, deception.
māsa-, s. m., month.
māsika-, a., monthly, mensual.
mitra-, s. n., friend; °*drohin-*, a., betraying a friend.
mukta-, s. *muc-*.
mukha-, s. n., mouth, face, head.
mugdha-, a., stupid, simple.
muc-, VI *muñcati*, X, loosen, liberate; with *nis*, X, set free.
muṇḍa-, a., shaved, bald, having the head shaved.
mudita-, a., glad.
muni-, s. m., a (silent) seer and wise man.
mumūrṣu-, s. *mṛ-*.
muṣ-, IX, steal, rob.
muṣṭi-, s. m. f., fist.
muhus, *muhur*, *muhuḥ*, repeatedly.
muhūrta-, s. m n., hour.
mūḍha-, a., foolish.
mūrkha-, a., stupid; s. m., fool.
mūrtimat-, a., incarnate.
mūla-, s. n., root; *unmūlayati*, root out, eradicate.
mūṣika-, s. m., mouse.
mṛ-, *mriyate*, die.
mṛga-, s. m., wild animal, gazelle, stag.
mṛgayā-, s. f., hunting, chase.
mṛj-, *mārṣṭi*, *mārjati*, rub off; with *sam*, rub, sweep.
mṛta- (*mṛ-*), a., dead.
mṛd-, IX, crush, destroy.
mṛś- with *vi*, VI and X, consider (frequently written with *ṣ*).
medas-, s. n., fat.
medinī-, s. f., earth.
meṣa-, s. m., ram.
mokṣa-, s. m., release.
moha-, s. m., insanity, deception, delusion.
mohana-, a., deluding.
mohin-, a., confusing.
maunavrata-, a., who observes the vow of silence.

ya-, rel. pron., who, which.
yakṣa-, s. m., Yakṣa (name of a class of mytholog. beings).
yajña-, s. m., sacrifice.
yat-, *yatate*, strive for.
yatas, whence; in consequence of which; where; since, because.
yatna-, s. m., exertion, effort.
yatra, where, whither (relat.).
yathā, as, that, so that.
yathākālam, adv. (§ 113), at the right time, opportunely.
yathārtha-, a., right, appropriate.
yad; pron. § 50; conj. that; because.
yadā, when, if.
yadi, if, in case.
yantrita-, a., shot by a tightly tensed bow.
yam, *yacchati*, with *ni*, restrain, hold back, strengthen, hold fast; with *pra*, lend, bestow.
Yama-, s. m., the god of the kingdom of the dead.
yaśas-, s. n., reputation, dignity, fame.

yasmād (abl. s. n. § 50), since, because.
yā-, II, go; with *ā*, come to; with *sam-ā*, come hither (together); with *pra*, depart, set out, journey to.
yāc-, I, request.
yātrā-, s. f., journey.
yāvat-, a., as great; adv., so long as, so far as, as long, as soon as, while; *yāvan na*, before.
yugapad, adv., simultaneously.
yuj-, VII, X, yoke; *yujyate*, it is right, fitting; with *pra*, X, discharge, shoot; with *sam*, provide with.
yuddha-, s. n., battle.
yudh-, s. f., battle, combat.
yudh-, *yudhyate*, fight; X, cause to fight, fight against.
yuvatī-, s. f., young woman.
yūtha-, s. m., troop, herd.
yoktra-, s. n., cord, rope.
yogin-, a., s. m., devoted to Yoga, Yogin.
yogya-, a., fitting, fit.
yauvana-, s. n., youth.

rakṣ-, *rakṣati*, p.p.p. *rakṣita-*, protect; with *pari*, protect.
rakṣaka-, s. m., guard.
rakṣaṇa-, s. n., protecting, preserving.
rakṣas-, s. n., (nocturnal) demon.
rajaka-, s. m., washerman.
rajanī-, s. f., night.
rajju-, s f., cord, rope.
raṇa-, s. n., battle.
rata-, a., finding pleasure in (l.).
ratna-, s. n., jewel.
ratha-, s. m., war-chariot.
rabh-, I, with *ā*, begin, undertake.
ram-, IV mid., take pleasure in; with *vi*, stop, calm down.
ramya-, a., graceful, charming, beauteous.
ramaṇīya-, a., delightful.
rasa-, s. m., juice, fluid.
rahita-, a., deserted by (+ instr.).
rākṣasa-, a., devilish; s.m., monster, demon.
rājan-, s. m., king.
rājaputrī-, s. f., princess.
rājya-, s. n., dominion, rule.
rātri-, s. f., night.
rādh-, with *apa*, IV, transgress, be guilty.
ripu-, s. m., enemy.
ru-, II, roar, bellow, howl.
ruci-, s. f., taste.
rud-, II (§ 64 VI), *roditi*, cry, weep, shed tears.
Rudra-, = Śiva, name of a god.
rudhira-, s. n., blood.
ruh-, I, climb up, grow; with *ā*, climb.
rūpa-, s. n., figure, form, beauty.
rūpaka-, s. m., rupee.
rūpavat-, *rūpāḍhya-*, a., beautiful.
°*rūpin-*, having the figure . . .
roṣa-, s. m., anger.
raudra-, a., frightful.

lakṣ-, X, perceive, notice, observe.
Lakṣmī-, s. f., the goddess of fortune.
lag-, I, attach oneself to.
laghu-, a., light.
laghutā-, s. f., insignificance, frivolity, small repute.
lajjā-, s. f., modesty, shame.

labh-, I mid., get.
lamb-, *lambate*, hang down, hang upon; with *ava*, caus., hang; with *ā*, seize, submit.
likh-, VI, scratch; with *vi*, scratch, tear up.
lih, II *leḍhi*, lick; intens. constantly lick; with *ava*, lick on.
lī-, I, cling to, snuggle up to, attach oneself to.
līlā-, s. f., play; *līlayā*, without any effort.
lok-, X, look; with *ava*, look (at); with *ā*, regard; with *vi*, look at, consider, catch sight of.
loka-, s. m., world, people.
lokātman-, s. m., the soul of the world.
locana-, s. n., eye.
lomaharṣaṇa-, a., causing the hair to stand on end.

vaktumanas-, a., intending to say.
vac-, say, name; with *prati*, answer.
vacana-, s. n., word.
vacas-, s. n., word.
vajra-, s. m., thunderbolt.
vañc-, X, deceive; p. p. part. *vañcita-*.
vaḍavā-, s. f., mare.
vaṇij-, s. m., merchant.
°*vat*, adv. suffix, like, as.
vad-, *vadati*, speak, say; caus., cause to sound; with *abhi*, X, address, greet.
vadhū-, s. f., woman, wife.
vana-, s. n., forest.
vanaspati-, s. m., tree.
vanaukas-, s. m., inhabitant of the forest, anchorite.
vanya-, a., living in the forest, growing in the forest.
vapus-, s. n., figure, body.
vam-, I, spit, spew out.
vayas-, s. n., (youthful) age.
vara-, a., most excellent, best.
I *vara-*, s. m., wish.
II *vara-*, s. m., suitor, husband.
varāha-, s. m., wild boar.
varjita-, a., to whom something is lacking, free from, without.
varṇa-, s. m., color.
vartin-, a., present, existent, current.
varṣa-, s. m. n., rain; year.
vallī-, s. f., climbing plant.
vaśa-, s. m., will, wish; *vaśāt*, in consequence . . ., by virtue of.
I *vas-*, *vaste*, dress, clothe.
II *vas-*, I, dwell, lodge; caus., shelter; with *ni*, tarry, live; with *pra*, set out; with *prati*, dwell.
vasudhā-, s. f., earth, land.
vahni-, s. m., fire.
vā, or.
vākya-, s. n., speech, words.
vāc-, s. f., word, speech.
vāñch-, wish.
vāṇī-, s. f., speech.
vāta-, s. m., wind.
vāda-, s. m., expression; sound, call, ring.
vānara-, s. m., ape.
vāyavya-, a., pertaining to the wind or to the god of the wind.
vāyu-, s. m., wind.
vāri-, s. n., water.
vāsin-, a., dwelling.
Vāsuki-, s. m., a prince of serpents.

vāhana-, s. n., chariot.
vikraya-, s. m., sale.
vikhyāta-, a., famous.
vijara-, a., not aging.
vijñapti-, s. f., the address of an inferior to a superior; request.
vittavat-, a., rich.
vid-, *vindati*, find; *vidyate*, there is (are).
vidyā-, s. f., knowledge, teaching, science.
vidvat- (p.p. act. of *vid-*), knowing.
vidhi-, s. m., method, way; rule; fate.
vidhura-, a., disagreeable, unfavorable.
vinaṣṭa-, p.p.p. of *naś-* + *vi*.
vinā, without (with acc. and instr.).
vipatti-, s. f., misfortune.
vipad-, s. f., misfortune.
vipaścit-, a., wise.
vipra-, s. m., Brahman.
vibudha-, s. m., god.
vibhāga-, s. m., part.
vimāna-, s. m. n., palace; a chariot traveling through the air.
viraha-, s. m., separation.
virahita-, a., abandoned, deprived.
vivardhin-, a., increasing.
viveka-, s. m., correct discrimination, judgment.
viś-, VI, go into; with *ā*, p.p.p., filled with; with *upa*, sit down; caus., seat someone; with *sam-upa*, sit down; with *pra*, enter.
viśālākṣa-, a., great-eyed.
viśeṣa-, s. m., distinction, manner; —°, a definite . . .; *viśeṣena*, especially.
viśrabdha-, a., trusting, without hesitation.
viśvasta-, a., full of confidence.
viśvāsa-, s. m., confidence.
viṣa-, s. n., poison.
viṣaṇṇa-, a., disconcerted.
vismaya-, s. m., astonishment.
vihaga-, s. m., bird.
vihāra-, s. m. n., monastery.
vīra-, s. m., hero.
vīrudh-, s. f., herb, plant.
vīryavat-, a., mighty, able.
I *vṛ-*, V, cover; with *sam-ā*, cover; with *ni*, X, hold back; restrain.
II *vṛ-*, IX, *vṛṇīte*, choose, wish; *varaṃ vṛ-*, wish a wish.
vṛkṣa-, s. m., tree.
vṛt-, I, *vartate*, become, be; X, live by (with instr.); with *abhi*, set about or upon; with *pra*, arise, begin, set about, proceed; (with dat.), submit; with *vi*, roll.
vṛthā, indecl., uselessly, vainly.
vṛddha-, a., old.
vṛdh-, I, increase, flourish.
vṛṣṭi-, s. f., rain.
vega-, s. m., impetuosity, haste, rashness.
veda-, s. m., knowledge, Veda.
vedanā-, s. f., pain.
velā-, s. f., moment, period of time.
veśman-, s. n., house.
vai, particle of asseveration.
vaidheya-, a., stupid; s., blockhead.
vaihāyasa-, a., standing in the air; s. n., air, open space.
vyakta-, a., obvious, manifest.
vyagratā-, s. f., occupation.

vyadh-, *vidhyati*, pierce; with *prati*, shoot (at).
vyasana-, s. n., passionate devotion, vice.
vyākulatva-, s. n., alarm, excitement.
vyāghra-, s. m., tiger.
vyādha-, s. m., hunter.
vyādhi-, s. m., illness.
vyāyāma-, s. m., bodily exertion; battle.
vyāla-, s. m., beast of prey; snake.
vraj-, I, go.
vrata-, s. n., vow.

śak-, V, be able.
śakala-, s. m. n., chip, splinter, small piece.
śakta-, a., being able.
śakti-, s. f., power, ability.
Śaṅkara-, = Rudra-Siva.
śaṅkha-, s. m., sea shell.
śata-, s. n., hundred.
Śatakratu-, = Indra.
śatadhā, hundredfold.
śatru-, s. m., enemy.
śanaiḥ (*śanaiḥ*), slowly, gradually.
śabda-, s. m., tone, sound, word, speech.
śam-, with *pra*: *praśamita-*, annihilated, killed.
śara-, s. m., arrow.
śaraṇa-, s. n., shelter, refuge.
śarīra-, s. n., body.
śarman-, s. n., protection, rescue, preservation.
Śarva- = Rudra-Śiva.
śava-, s. m. n., corpse.
śastra-, s. n., sword, knife.
śākhā-, s. f., branch, bough.
śādvala-, s. n., lawn.
śānti-, s. f., rest, peace of mind; the absence of an evil effect and the ceremony directed thereto.
śāntika-, s. n., preventative measure.
śāpa-, s. m., curse.
Śārṅgin-, = Viṣṇu.
śārdūla-, s. m., tiger.
śālā-, s. f., hall, room, stable.
śās-, II, prevail over, rule.
śāstra-, s. n., science, textbook.
śikhara-, s. n., peak, summit.
śikhin-, s. m., fire.
śiras-, s. n., head.
śilā-, s. f., stone, crag.
śiloccaya-, s. m., mountain, hill.
śiva-, a., friendly, blessed.
śiṣ-, VII, leave remaining; with *vi*: *viśiṣyate*, be worth more (than: instr.).
śiṣya-, s. m., pupil.
śī-, II, mid., lie, recline.
śīghra-, a., quick, rapid.
śīta-, a., cold.
śīla-, s. n., (noble) character; habit (frequently as the 2nd member of a comp., with that which has become habit for one, for which one possesses a special inclination or ability, in the 1st member).
śuc-, I, mourn.
śuci-, a., pure, clean.
śunī-, s. f., female dog.
śubha-, a., beautiful, good, favorable.
śuṣ-, X, with *upa*, dry up, dessicate.
śūnya-, a., empty.
śūla-, s. n., spit, spike, spear.

śūra-, s. m., hero.
śṛgāla-, s. m., jackal.
śeṣa-, s. m. n., rest; °-, a., of which only . . . is left.
śaila-, s. m., crag, mountain.
śoka-, s. m., grief.
śoṣa-, s. m., drying up.
śoṣaṃ gam-, become dry.
śmaśāna-, s. n., cemetery.
śyena-, s. m., falcon.
śrama-, s. m., trouble.
śrāddha-, s. n., funeral feast and gifts.
śrī-, s. f., beauty, success.
śru-, V *śṛṇoti*, hear; caus., inform; des. *śuśrūṣate*, obey.
śreṣṭha-, superl., most excellent.
śreṣṭhin-, s. m., guild master.
śloka-, s. m., strophe.
śvan-, s. m., dog.
śvāśura-, a., belonging to the father-in-law.

ṣaṭ-, six.
ṣaṣṭi-, s. f., sixty.

sa°, with . . .
°*saṃkāśa-*, resembling . . .
saṃkruddha-, a., angered, irritated.
saṃgati-, s. f., meeting.
saṃgraha-, s. m., gathering.
saṃgrāma-, s. m., combat, battle.
saṃjāta-, s. *jan-*.
saṃjīvana-, a., vivifying, animating.
saṃtāpa-, s. m., heat; pain, remorse, repentance.
saṃnidhāna-, s. n., nearness.
saṃnihita-, a., situated in the vicinity.
saṃpatti-, s. f., success.
saṃpanna-, (*pad-*) a., finished, provided with.
saṃparipālana-, s. n., protection, protecting.
saṃpiṣṭa-, s. *piṣ-*.
saṃprāpta-, s. *āp-*.
saṃbandhin-, s. m., relative.
saṃbhrānta-, a., confused, excited.
saṃmārjat-, s. *mṛj-*.
saṃvatsara-, s. m., year.
saṃśaya-, s. m., doubt; *na s.* without doubt.
saṃśraya-, s. m., refuge, place of residence.
saṃśrita-, a., resting on, with reference to.
saṃskāra-, s. m., consummation of a sacrament, e.g., the burning of a corpse.
saṃskṛta-, a., prepared; correct.
°*saṃsthita-* (*sthā-*), a., having the shape of . . .; s. n., form, figure.
saṃhṛṣṭa-, a., glad.
sakala-, a., all, entire, whole.
sakāśa-, s. m., presence; abl. from . . .
sakṛt, once.
saktu-, s. m., grits, groats.
sakhi-, n. sing. *sakhā*, s. m., friend.
sakhī-, s. f., female friend.
saṅgha-, s. m., troop, crowd.
sajjīkṛ-, provide with a (bow) string.
sañj-, *sajati*, *sajyate*, *sajjate*, be attached to; with *ā*: p.p.p. *āsakta-*, attached to, occupied with.
sat-, pr. part. of *as-*, be; also: good.

satatam, continuously.
sattama-, s. *sat-*.
sattra-, s. n., a Soma celebration.
satya-, a., true; s. n., truth.
satyavacana-, s. n., promise.
satvaram, quickly, most hastily.
sad-, I, *sīdati*, sit; with *ava*, slacken, despair; with *ā*, X, arrive at something; *āsādya*, with consideration for, in accordance with:
sadā, always.
sanātana-, a., eternal, everlasting.
sanātha-, a., provided with.
saphala-, a., successful.
sabhya-, a., suited for society.
sama-, a., equal.
samaya-, s. m., point of time, period of time.
samara-, s. m. n., combat.
samasta-, a., whole.
samāgata-, a., s. *gam-* with *sam-ā*.
samāna-, a., equal.
samāpana-, s. n., finish, end.
samāpta- (*āp-*), a., s. n., finished.
samāhita- (*dhā-* with *sam-ā*), a., brought forth.
samīpa-, s. n., nearness, proximity, presence.
samudra-, s.m., sea.
samyak, adv., quite, properly, correctly.
Saramā-, s. f., name of the bitch of the gods.
saras-, s. n., pool, lake.
sarga-, s. m., creation, world, cosmos.
sarpa-, s. m., snake, serpent.
sarva-, a., whole, all, every.
sarvatra, everywhere.
sarvadā, always.
savitṛ-, s. m., sun.
saviśeṣam, quite exactly, preferably, excellently.
sasya-, s. n., farm produce, crop.
sah-, I endure (be able).
saha, with.
°*saha-*, a., enduring.
sahaja-, a., inborn, native to.
sahabhojana-, s. n., eating together.
sahas-, s. n., power.
sahasā, suddenly, immediately.
sahasra-, s. n., thousand.
sahasradhā, thousandfold.
sahāya-, s. m., companion.
sahita-, a., united (with instr.), together.
sāṃpratam, now.
sāṃyātrika-, s. m., seafarer, sailor.
sākṣāt, adv., before the eyes, manifestly; in person.
sādana-, s. n., seat, dwelling.
sādh-, X, accomplish, settle, carry out; bring into one's power.
sādhu-, a., good, right.
sāntva-, s. n., reconciliation.
Sārameya-, s. m., name of a dog; metron. of *Saramā-*.
sārasvata-, a., pertaining to the goddess of speech (Sarasvatī).
sārdham, together with (i.).
siṃha-, s. m., lion.
sic-, *siñcati*, sprinkle.
siddha-, a., attained.
su°, well, quite.
sukha-, a., pleasant; s. n., joy.
sutā-, s. f., daughter.
sudharmātman-, a., quite virtuous.
sudhārmika-, a., fulfilling one's duties exactly.

sundara-, a., beautiful.
supta-, s. *svap-*.
subhāṣita-, s. n., a fine utterance.
sumanas-, a., intelligent.
sura-, s. m., god.
suvarcas-, a., full of vigor.
suvarṇa-, s. n., gold.
suhṛd-, s. m., friend.
sūrya-, s. m., sun.
sṛj-, VI, let loose, hurl, utter; with *ud*, give up, disregard; with *vi*, discharge, let loose, utter.
sṛṣṭi-, s. f., universe, world, cosmos.
senā-, s. f., army.
sev-, I, inhabit; serve; honor; cherish, practice, devote oneself to.
sainika-, s. m., soldier.
sainya-, s. n., army.
skandha-, s. m., shoulder.
stambha-, s. m., post, column.
stu-, II § 64 VIII, praise.
strī-, s. f., woman.
sthā-, I, stand; with acc., carry out something; with *anu*, pursue, be engaged in, carry out something; with *vi-ava*, stop, be settled, be; with *ā*, resort to, take up; indulge in; with *ud*, arise; with *sam-ud*, rise up; with *upa*, be available or at one's disposal; with *sam-upa*, fall to one's lot; with *pra*, set out, depart; with *sam*, tarry.
sthita-, s. *sthā-*; also: present.
sthira-, a., firm, resistant.
snā- II, bathe.
snuṣā-, s. f., daughter-in-law.
sneha-, s. m., friendship, love.
spṛś-, VI, touch; with *upa*, bathe.
sphaṭ-, X, tear up; p.p.p. burst, sprung.
sma, slightly asseverative particle; cf. § 115 I.
smita-, s. n., smiling, smile.
smṛ-, I, remember; with *vi*, forget.
sva-, a., own, inherent.
svap-, II, *svapiti*, sleep; verb. adj. *supta*.
svayam, self.
svara-, s. m., sound, voice.
svarga-, s. m., heaven.
svasṛ-, s. f., sister.
svādu-, a., tasty, sweet.
svānta-, s. n., the heart (as seat of the emotions).
svāmin-, s. m., lord, master.

haṃsa-, s. m., goose, gander.
hata- (verb. adj. of *han-*), killed, slain.
han-, II, strike, hit, kill; with *abhi*, strike, hit, afflict; with *abhi-ā*, strike; with *ni*, strike, attack; with *prati*, strike back, kill; with *sam*, destroy, ger., together.
hanta, come on! go to it!
haya-, s. m., horse.
Hara-, = Śiva.
Hari-, = Viṣṇu.
harṣa-, m., joy.
havis-, s. n., § 34, sacrificial offering.
has-, *hasati*, laugh; with *apa*, X, laugh about something; with *pra*, laugh out.
hasta-, s. m., hand.
hastin-, s. m., elephant.

Hastināpura, s. n., name of a town or city.
hā-, III, leave; *hīyate*, vanish, lose; with *apa-ā*, s. *apāhāya*.
hātavya- grdv. (§ 116 VII), what should be avoided.
hālāhala-, s. n., a very strong poison.
hi, for, surely.
hita-, verb. adj. of *dhā-*, good, excellent; s. n., welfare.
hitvā (to *hā-*), § 117, also: with omission of.
himavat-, a., (very) snowy.
hiraṇya-, s. n., gold.
hīna-, a., free of, lacking (with instr.).
hīyate, s. *hā-*.
hu-, III, pour into the fire, sacrifice.
hṛ-, I, take, steal; with *apa*, take away; with *ā*, bring, give; with *vi-ā*, speak; with *ud*, remove, eliminate, delete.
hṛta-, a., stolen, robbed.
hṛd-, s. n., heart.
hṛdaya-, s. n., heart.
Hṛṣīkeśa-, = Viṣṇu.
he, vocative interj., hi!
hemanta-, s. m., winter.
hve- I, *hvayati*, call.